## PRAISE FOR BRAD STEIGER's TOTEMS

"Borrowing from Amerindian shamanic traditions, Steiger presents an area and techniques for personal development that will be totally new to most readers. With personal experiences and fascinating details he guides the reader into new and productive spiritual dimensions."

—Frank C. Tribbe, editor of *Spiritual Frontiers*

"Totems have played an important role in many native traditions. Although there are no universal meanings for totem animals and birds, the variety of meanings assigned to them is vividly described by Brad Steiger in this entertaining book."

—Stanley Krippner, Ph.D., co-author of *Spiritual Dimensions of Healing*

"Seekers will find *Totems* replete with personal experiences—those of Native American shamans along with those of ordinary people. The book not only fully explains the meaning behind totems as a door to the unconscious, but it presents down-to-earth basic instructions and exercises to lead you on a quest to transformation and self-empowerment. It reveals how all of nature, including humankind, is connected at an invisible level. This is a timely and wonderful book."

—Raymond Buckland, author of *Doors to Other Worlds*

# TOTEMS

## THE TRANSFORMATIVE POWER OF
## YOUR PERSONAL ANIMAL TOTEM

### Brad Steiger

HarperSanFrancisco

*An Imprint of* HarperCollins*Publishers*

To the memory of Glenn McWane,
who left the Earth Mother on the wings of his totem guide,
the eagle, in January of 1996.

Special thanks to Twylah Nitsch, Julia C. White, Sharon Rammon,
Tara Buckland, Laura Day, Esther Hamel, Beverly Hale Watson,
L. Dean Woodruff, Tara Sutphen, Lawrence Kennedy,
Sandra Sitzmann, Mary Elizabeth Thunder,
Lorraine Darr, and Sherry Hansen Steiger.

A TREE CLAUSE BOOK

HarperSanFrancisco and the author, in associaton with The Basic Foundation, a
not-for-profit organization whose primary mission is reforestation, will facilitate the
planting of two trees for every one tree used in the manufacture of this book.

HarperCollins Web Site: http://www.harpercollins.com
HarperCollins®, ®, and HarperSanFrancisco™ and A TREE CLAUSE BOOK® are
trademarks of HarperCollins Publishers Inc.

*Library of Congress Cataloging-in-Publication Data*
Steiger, Brad.
Totems : the transformative power of your animal totem / Brad Steiger. – 1st ed.
ISBN 0–06–251425–3(pbk.)
1. Animals—Religious aspects.   2. Totems.   3. Spiritual life.   I. Title.
BL325.A6S74   1997     291.2'12—dc20     96–4898

01 ❖ RRDH 10

# Contents

1. Our Animal Companions on Turtle Island    1

2. Receive the Power of Your Animal Totem    15

3. Entering Shamanic Time    41

4. Going on Spirit Journeys    55

5. Catching and Retrieving Dream Teachings    71

6. The Sacred Force Behind All Magic    85

7. Praying for Strength and Guidance    97

8. Avoiding the Horrid Things of Darkness    115

9. The Healing Powers of Totems    125

10. Receiving Initiation into Higher Awareness    139

Totem Animal Dictionary    151

Bibliography    213

# CHAPTER I

# Our Animal Companions on Turtle Island

I JOINED THE OTHERS in the teaching circle with Grandmother Twylah in the original Seneca longhouse of the old Buffalo Creek Reservation and listened to her tell us about the harmony that once existed among all living things in the beautiful forests of our Turtle Island.

Before any human beings there was the Great Mystery. After preparing the Sun and Moon and Water and setting them into place, the Great Mystery made patterns for all things that were to be born and arranged for all happenings that were to occur.

Then the Great Mystery prepared Nature Land, where all things were to mingle in harmony, and the Great Mystery created the plants and all the creatures that swam, crawled, walked, and flew. Gifts were bestowed upon them, with abilities to learn lessons from one another.

All things belong to the Great Mystery. For this reason, the same Spirit is in everything that breathes, senses, hears, tastes, smells, and sees. The inhabitants of Nature Land are aware of the Great Mystery through the whisperings that speak through the mind.

The ancestors of our people sensed a powerful force all around them. Some were able to feel the force; others were able to see it. They called the force *Swen-i-o,* the Great Mystery.

The lessons that nature taught set a pattern for the people to follow. The Seneca soon learned that each person must find a way to fit into this pattern in order to experience a sense of happiness. In the atmosphere of the forest, they recognized the presence of the Great Mystery. Its force penetrated into every soul, making every soul a part of it.

As they learned the unspoken language of the inhabitants who live in the forest, the Seneca understood the necessity for living in harmony with self and with nature.

They accepted the kinship of all creatures and all plants of nature.

They believed all creatures and plants were equal in the sight of nature, each performing its specific talents according to its abilities.

Whenever the Seneca fell out of balance with nature, they caused conditions of discord. When the Seneca developed spiritual equality and a life of spiritual balance, they became a mature people of wisdom.

The Seneca taught their children the importance of identifying themselves with all creatures and plants of nature. They learned the differences between themselves and the creatures, but they understood that it was the same Spirit flowing through all of them.

## ALL OF NATURE IS IN US

Understanding the sanctity of nature and having a reverence for life begins with the recognition that we humans are but one species of living beings. All living things are the Great Mystery's sacred creations, endowed with spirit, consciousness, and intelligence.

In the Oracle of Atsuta, an expression of the path of Shinto, it is written: "Regard heaven as your father, earth as your mother, and all things as your brothers and sisters."

In his thought-provoking book *Recovering the Soul: A Scientific and Spiritual Search*, Dr. Larry Dossey theorizes about the existence of a universal mind that connects human beings, animals, and all living things. From the very beginning of human evolution, Dr. Dossey suggests, it has made "good biological sense that a nonlocal, psychological communion might have developed between humans and animals as an asset to survival . . . [that] . . . nature in its wisdom would, in fact, have designed a mind that envelops all creatures great and small."

To fully understand and embrace the concept of a "nonlocal mind" requires a genuine humility that enables us to know deeply "that we may be on a similar footing with all the rest of God's creatures."

The Bhagavad Gita (6:28–32) states that those who touch the Godhead and free themselves from the burden of evil see "the Self in every creature and all creation in the Self."

In *Shamanic Voices: A Survey of Visionary Narratives,* Joan Halifax quotes Petagna Yuha Mani's statement: "As my brother Lame Deer has said, all of nature is in us, all of us is in nature. That's as it should be."

Today, Grandmother Twylah, the Repositor of Wisdom for her tribe, still teaches her students the Seneca practice of going into the Silence of solitude to regain the feeling of belonging to nature, of being at one with the Great Mystery, and of being in harmony with all of nature's creatures.

To enter the Silence, in Grandmother's words, is "to be enchanted by the Great Mystery." It is truly a magical process by which serious-minded students are able to elevate their consciousness to the spiritual realm, where visions of the past, present, and future live in an existence independent of our material world. This dimension exists in the Eternal Now, thus making it older than Time and newer than our next heartbeat.

## Draw Upon Ancient Wisdom Through Your Animal Totem

One of the most effective methods of drawing upon the power of this ancient wisdom is to regain the awareness that you are once again fitting into the pattern of nature and that you are living in harmony with all creatures. And one of the quickest ways to truly understand that it is the very same Spirit that flows through you and through all other beings is to learn the proper use of animal symbology in the creation of your own personal totem.

Among the Medicine teachings of the traditional Native Americans, the totem represents the physical form of one's spirit helper, his or her guardian or guide.

As Medicine Hawk and Grey Cat have said, "While the Great Mystery lives in everything, animate and inanimate, it also exists as itself. It is above us and at the same time is us. It is not a 'God' in the European's sense of God. Neither are the totems 'godlings,' separate pantheistic deities. However, there may in some ways be a comparison to the concept of the guardian angel."

Or as one of my own students once suggested during a Medicine seminar, "The totem entity is kind of like a spirit guide or guardian angel that presents itself to you on the earth plane in the form of an animal."

However one wishes to identify and name the animal form that represents one's spirit helper, I can promise that to do so will create a spiritual-psychological mechanism that will bring about great personal transformation and manifest an extended sphere of awareness in an ever-expanding reality construct.

"You must learn to live in harmony with everything around you," said Amoneeta Sequoyah, a great Cherokee shaman. "If you let the animals know that you mean good, they'll be good to you. They will be your helpers."


## Activating Cosmic Memory

Robert Davidson is an internationally known artist who is giving new life to the art forms that represent the Haida, the native people of northern Canada and Alaska. Although the ancient style has been praised for its power and beauty since the late eighteenth century, few masters remained when Davidson was born in 1946.

Since he didn't even know that he was a Native American until an uncle informed him of his heritage when he was a boy of eleven, how was it that Davidson was able to absorb the ancient process that has allowed him to create carvings, prints, sculptures, paintings, jewelry, and totem poles that have won critical acclaim around the globe?

In 1980, when he was thirty-four, Davidson began learning the traditional songs that his grandmother had sung. He helped found the Rainbow Dancers and began to carve animal masks for the performers to wear at special ceremonies. He found himself bestowing a new respect on the cultural and spiritual attributes of the salmon, the eagle, the raven, and the bear.

He learned that the Haida believe that everything is human. In their own supernatural world, creatures look exactly like human beings. They only put on their animal forms when they are in our world.

Early in his work, Davidson discovered that the frog came to symbolize his spirit helper. He didn't know why exactly—but the image of a frog kept showing up at important moments in his life.

By continuing to utilize the traditional ways and by personally tapping into the kinds of cultural experiences that his ancestors had, Davidson began to see clearly that culture is really a process, not something frozen in time.

"We all have that cosmic memory," he said. "We are all connected to our cultural past in some way."*

Through his dreams and visions, Davidson says that he has visited the spirit world and has seen that the images there are alive. He has then returned to the physical world and employed those powerful images to enrich his life, his art, and his personal relationships.

## CONNECTIONS TO OUR CULTURAL PAST

Although we may not all be artists seeking vivid images from other dimensions of reality to inspire our creativity, we may all profit from

* Quoted by W. S. Kowinski, *Smithsonian* (January 1995).

the personal empowerment that can be derived from connecting with the cultural experiences of our ancestors and becoming one with our own unique cosmic memories. Humankind, wherever on the globe its myriad expressions have chosen to dwell, has the same spiritual ancestry, receives the same revelations from Higher Intelligence, and expresses itself in similar ritual acts, whose origins may be but dim memories in the collective unconscious. Robert Davidson is absolutely correct when he states that we are all connected to our cultural past in some way.

And in each of our cultural pasts, our ancestors employed animal totems. We still do so today. Take a moment to look at the names of local sports teams and all the Tigers, Lions, and Bears that occupy stadiums on weekends. Or consider contemporary religious expressions, such as the images of the Lamb of God, the Dove of the Holy Spirit, or the Lion of Judah, which inspire devotion on the Sabbath. These totem animals were created to serve the group psyche, and it is extremely doubtful that they can satisfy your own need for a personal spirit helper, an individual symbol of comfort, or a spiritual-psychological mechanism to manifest awareness.

In their *Warriors of the Rainbow*, William Willoya and Vinson Brown state that the traditional Native Americans used the animal spirit as a tool in reaching the Source of the World and in purifying the soul:

"The great, pure-hearted chiefs . . . achieved their spiritual power by the most difficult self-discipline, fasting, and prayer, including the utter emptying of the heart of all earthly desires and tuning on the inner ear to the whispers of the wilderness. This was not idol worship . . . but something far deeper and more wonderful, the understanding of the Spirit Being that manifests itself in all living things."

As Grandmother Twylah and others have taught us, the traditional Native American sees the work of the Great Mystery in every expression of life upon the Earth Mother. Sadly, for far too long, such a belief was misinterpreted by the invading European, who, in the early days of conquest and mission work, saw the native people interacting with their totem animals and became convinced that the Amerindian worshiped idols and a hierarchy of many gods.

While the traditionalist does indeed believe that the Great Mystery manifests itself in a variety of forms, it must be understood that to see the expression of Deity in everything is not the same as seeing everything as Deity. Regretfully, only a few of the white invaders were able to discern the distinction between acknowledging a Supreme Being's work in all of life and worshiping elemental forces.

"You didn't try to understand our prayers," Walking Buffalo complained in *Tatana Mani, Walking Buffalo of the Stonies*. "You said we were worshipping idols. Without understanding, you condemned us as lost souls ... We saw the Great Spirit's work in everything ... Sometimes we approached him through these things ... I think we have a true belief in the Supreme Being, a stronger faith than that of most whites who have called us pagans."

For those early missionaries who truly listened and paid attention to the shamans, there was never any misconception that the native people were worshiping animals as deities. David Brainerd, who began his mission in 1742, stated in his *Life and Travels*, "They [the Lenape, also known as Delaware] do not suppose a divine power essential ... in these creatures, but that some invisible beings ... communicate to these animals a great power, and so make these creatures the immediate authors of good to certain persons."

Writing circa 1779, David Zeisberger, a Moravian missionary who had years of personal contact with numerous tribes and translated scriptural texts for the Algonguin, stated: "They believe that there is an Almighty Being who has created heaven and earth and man and all things else. This they have learned from their ancestors."

Dallas Chief Eagle, a shaman of the Teton Sioux, once told me, "The Great Mystery made nature for us to use and preserve, but nature also imposes obligations upon us. We are only passing through life on the way to the spirit worlds of our ancestors. Always remember that you have to know what you are in order to feel the Great Mystery in nature—and it is only through nature that you can gain communion with the Holy Mystery."

Latvian ethnologist Ivar Lissner stated in *Man, God and Religion* that his seventeen years of expeditions among the Tungus, Polynesians, Melasians, Australian Aborigines, Ainus, Japanese, Chinese, Mongols, and North American tribes demonstrated to him quite clearly that totemism is not religion. While all these diverse people lived in a world filled with animate beings, they all believed in a single supreme deity.

"Since the whole of our terrestrial and celestial environment is animated and activated by a force beyond our ken, animism is really a part of each and every one of us," he comments. "The closer to nature man is, the more strongly he feels this. Thus the number of animists of varying complexions runs not into millions, but hundreds of millions."

### RECEIVING THE SPIRIT HELPER DURING THE VISION QUEST

The spirit helper is usually received during the vision quest. Before initiates embark upon their ordeal, tribal elders and Medicine priests tutor them for many weeks on what to expect and what is expected of them. Most important, they are made to understand that while they are on their quest, they are to fast, exhaust their physical bodies, and pray to the Great Mystery at least three times a day, asking that their spirit guide appear to them.

One of my spiritual mentors, a man who was reared in the Winnebago tradition, told me that the shamans advised his group of supplicants that after a few days on the quest a forest creature would be likely to approach them, as if to offer itself as a guide. A friendly chipmunk might nudge against their legs; an inquisitive crow might land on their shoulders; an especially curious deer might come forward to sniff at their faces.

The initiates were forewarned by the tribal elders that the temptation to accept the first animal that approached as one's spirit helper would be great; but if they were able to endure continued hunger and exposure, the Great Mystery would be certain to send them a more powerful spirit helper, one especially destined for the individual. The Medicine priest instructed the supplicants to thank each animal for its coming and to tell it of its beauty, strength, and intelligence, but to also inform it that they sought one even greater.

If one endured, according to some traditionalists, the true spirit helper would appear as if it were glowing, as though it were composed primarily of light.

As my mentor told me, "I don't think there was any way that we could have fooled the tribal elders. They knew when we had a true and real experience.

"One important thing we were taught: We must never call upon our guide until we had exhausted every bit of physical energy and mental resource possible. Then, after we had employed every last ounce of our own reserve, we might call upon our spirit helper and it would appear."

## INNER GUIDES AND ANIMAL TOTEMS

C. G. Jung wrote in his *Memories, Dreams, Reflections* that throughout his life he enjoyed conversations with his inner guide, whom he named Philemon. To the brilliant psychoanalyst, Philemon represented superior insight. Although Jung saw the entity as a "mysterious figure," he also said that Philemon was as real to him as if he were a living personality: "I went walking up and down the garden with him, and to me he was what the Indians call a guru."

I received my principal totem animal in August of 1972 when Twylah Nitsch did me the great honor of adopting me as her son into the Wolf Clan of the Seneca and initiating me into the Wolf Clan Medicine Lodge. My adoptive name is Hat-yas-swas (He Who Testifies), and I was charged with continuing to seek out and to share universal truths.

I feel very comfortable with the wolf as my personal totem and spirit helper. Wolves and/or dogs have often appeared in significant dreams to warn me of impending crises and to present me with symbols that have aided me in solving very troublesome problems.

Not long after I had accepted the wolf as my spirit helper, Sun Bear, the great Chippewa Medicine Priest, pointed out to me that according to the Medicine Wheel and his visions, together with those of his Medicine helper, Wabun, my birth sign indicated that the cougar was also one of my spirit helpers. This, too, felt correct.

I have since been directed through my own dreams, visions, and mystical experiences to accept the owl, the frog, and the dog, a guide in its own right, as additional spirit helpers and totem animals. I have learned to appreciate the marvelous truth in the following passage from the Book of Job (12:7–8): "Ask the animals, and they will teach you, or the birds of the air, and they will tell you; or speak to the earth, and it will teach you, or let the fish of the sea inform you."

Among many traditional Native Americans, the totem is a symbol of the name of the sacred progenitor, which stands as the surname of the family. Ancient legends tell of the Great Mystery transforming certain members of the bear family, the deer family, the wolf family, the turtle family, and so on, into two-legged humans, thus shaping the genesis of the various tribal clans.

Lest we of European ancestry should find this custom quaint or amusing, let us stop one moment to consider how universal is the practice of naming a family after a particular animal. I live in a very small Iowa community, yet even a quick flipping of the pages of our area telephone book easily produces the following last names of my neighbors—Bear, Beaver, Bird, Bull, Crane, Crow, Dolphin, Drake, Duck, Finch, Fish, Fox, Hawk, Lamb, Partridge, and Wolf. And that's not counting the German, Scandinavian, and Spanish surnames that translate into animal names.

## IDENTIFYING THE ANIMAL SPIRIT AND THE ANIMAL SELF

I had known for quite some time that my friends Lawrence Kennedy and Sandra Sitzmann of Polson, Montana, help their students to identify their animal selves and to analyze their animal characteristics and compatibility traits, but I had never asked them how they were able to identify their own animal totems.

Lawrence told me that he followed the Native American psycho-religious system known as Huna to determine the animal-self that matched his psychological, physiological, and emotional characteristics.

"The Huna beliefs of the traditional Hawaiian include concepts of a low-self, a high-self, and a middle-self, which are integrated as parts of the whole being," he said. "Each 'self' functions differently and yet harmoniously within the whole. There really are no divisions between these 'selves.' It is a separation of convenience only. The rational mind simply needs perimeters with which to operate due to past programming. The low-self can be addressed as an integrated and individual part of yourself, somewhat like addressing the individual personalities in a multiple personality situation."

According to Huna, Lawrence said, the reason why a particular animal becomes a predominant part of each individual is because the last stage of linear evolution before attaining humanhood is the animal kingdom. The lower part of "self" identifies with a particular animal from that very last stage of evolution before experiencing humanness.

Lawrence explained the technique that he used to discover his animal-self: "I created a mirror and/or a mental theater screen wherein my mind reflected back to me in a creative alpha state, similar to the way self-hypnosis is employed internally. After achieving the alpha mind control technique as a heightened state of awareness, I asked my animal-self to come forward. This state is a combination of the subconscious mind and your imagination, also known as lucid dreaming, where you are in control of the dream state."

Because Lawrence is the Leo sign in astrology, his mind was prepared to see a majestic lion appear on his "screen." Nothing happened—except for the appearance of two beady eyes that peered around his mental projection screen.

When Lawrence wondered what the holdup could be, he received a mental impression that the totem animal was something quite different from the lion that he had programmed himself to see.

But Lawrence was all right with that. "I had been previously instructed to accept lovingly whatever animal appeared, regardless of any pre-formed attitudes and judgments on the majestic value of an animal form. In other words, not all of us are eagles and lions. Other animals carry no lesser status, regardless of what humans have labeled them to be. There is no hierarchy involved among animals except for the symbolism that humans attach to them, such as a lion denoting royalty and strength."

At last Lawrence grew impatient. He told the shy totem animal that he did not care what it was. He just needed to see it. Please, he asked, make your appearance now.

"To my amazement, what I saw was a polar bear. He was not angry, not fierce-looking or frightening. As he keenly observed my initial reaction to him, I knew he fully sensed my fear on several levels, because I could not hide from the lower aspects of myself."

Finally, a soft, affectionate appreciation for the magnificent creature began to filter into Lawrence Kennedy's subconscious mind. "I began to feel a kinship with my newly accepted, lifelong part of myself. I was accepting and loving a part of myself. I marveled at this creation after I had viewed it in another light."

When he related his lion/polar bear experience to others, there was a concurrence that Lawrence was, indeed, a polar bear person. "For example, like the polar bear, I am large and tall in stature; and I have an extremely large chest without the very broad shoulders that one might automatically assume goes with it."

Using the Huna method, Lawrence helped Sandra Sitzmann to determine that her animal totems were the squirrel and the weasel. "Key words describing the squirrel are activity and preparedness," she said. "The squirrel scurries with busy energy and is social, communicative, observant, and imitative. My weasel totem is a very intelligent, graceful, solitary, and silent animal. Being social and solitary are not contradictory qualities, since both can exist at different times, depending upon the mood of the moment."

Lawrence and Sandra believe that we may have more than one animal totem. "However, there will be a predominant animal symbol acting as the primary power influence for you while other identified animal spirits will present a secondary representation," she explained. "We also discovered that animal-self mates are more or less compatible, depending upon the characteristics of their totems."

Sandra mused that at first glance she and Lawrence seem to be such extreme opposites that one might ask how and why they manage to remain together. The answer, she said, is seen through the eyes of some of their totem spirits and power animals: "Just visualize the intelligent, sleepy-slow, warm-n-cuddly polar bear and the bright, steadfast, active weasel. The roaring lion and the silently observant lamb. Wholeness can also be achieved by differences when the opposing qualities exist in harmony and balance through nonjudgment, acceptance, and lack of fear.

"More pragmatically," she continued, "Lawrence speaks and I write. He is objective and I am subjective. He dreams about architectural drawings and I attend to the details as we build foundations together. It takes two sides of a coin to create the whole, the balance, the unity. The ideal, of course, is to integrate both male and female aspects within one self to create the whole self—instead of splitting male and female attributes into duality. This wholeness is learned through the dance of relationships—even between a polar bear and a weasel. We have fought and embraced. We have cried and rejoiced. We have hated and we have loved. Even the most unlikely associations can become symbiotic when lovingly surrendering to aspects of each other's self."

## ALL CREATURES ARE RELATIVES

Donna Kay Barthelemy spent five years with a cross-cultural shaman who had been empowered by teachers from many different traditions, including Tibetan Buddhist, Hindu, Australian Aboriginal, as well as Native American. She writes that the shamanistic perspective regards each individual as a living system, which, in turn, is part of a series of increasingly complex systems:

"These include the family, which is part of the community; the tribe, which is part of the cosmos, etc. The human individual . . . has a place in the system of the cosmos, as do animals, plants, nature-spirits, and more powerful spiritual entities such as those known as 'the Grandfathers.'"

In the shamanistic system, Barthelemy continues, "All creatures are called 'relatives,' and are considered sisters, brothers, grandparents . . . Non-human relatives are considered 'people' and are prayed for . . . the birds (winged ones), the trees (tall standing people), the plants (green growing people), the four-leggeds, the creepy crawlies, as well as the two-leggeds."*

I am very much aware that the great majority of you who are reading this book were not born into clans or families that bear the names of animals. I also understand that few of you are likely to have undertaken a vision quest or a special class of instruction to learn the identity of your spirit helpers. Therefore, especially in chapter 2, I will draw upon the teachings that have been shared with me by powerful Medicine people from many different tribes and by shamans from many different traditions and provide a number of exercises and techniques that will enable each of you to receive an image of your spirit helper and allow you to choose your personal totem animal for self-empowerment.

* From "Shamanism as Living System," *The Quest* (Summer 1995).

Although I was adopted into the Seneca Wolf Clan and thus "inherited" the wolf as a totem animal, I was born an Iowan of Northern European ancestry. The Scandinavian and French traditions of my genetic ancestors are also very rich ones, filled with totemic animal symbolism. And so are the cultural traditions of the Irish, Scots, Germans, Italians, Jews, Spanish, Greeks, Chinese, Japanese, and so on, around the globe. By the time you finish reading this book, it will matter not if your ancestry is Seneca, Spanish, Scandinavian, Semitic, or Senegalese, you will be able to find the animal totem that will bring you self-empowerment, illumination, and spiritual transformation.

Hal Zina Bennett, Ph.D., writes in *Magical Blend* #16, 1987, that it is time for us to awaken to the fullest extent of our spiritual capacities: "It is a time not simply to learn from the inner guides of other people, but to learn to awaken and listen to one's own inner guides. Each one of us receives inner guidance every moment of our lives, and the guidance for each one of us is unique: tailored to our own lifepath. Because our lives are unique, our inner guidance is far more important and accurate than advice coming from others."

# CHAPTER 2

# Receive the Power of Your Animal Totem

WHEN SEVENTY-FOUR-YEAR-OLD Esther Hamel of St. Ignatius, Montana, shared her account of the spiritual gifts that she had received from her totem animals, she was still feeling pain from the death of her beloved husband of fifty-five years. Esther, who is of full German extraction, married a member of the Salish-Kootanai tribe, and she still lives on the beautiful Flathead Reservation in Montana.

Over the years, in addition to her roles as a wife, mother, and rancher, Esther has authored nine publications on art, horticulture, psychology, and government affairs. Recognized as a leader in community and national affairs, she was also the CEO of a research and development corporation, a publisher, a widely traveled lecturer, and the director of two national and international financial companies.

"Totems or 'spirit' animals are a Native American tradition, a symbol that all nature is connected at an unseen level," Esther said. "I can't remember when it was that I came to full awareness that the giraffe was my totem animal, but I had been collecting giraffes in statues, figurines, pins, poems, pictures, and articles for many years. When people would ask me why I collected giraffes, I would quip that not only did I admire the graceful, elegant elan with which they traversed their environment, but they reminded me of myself, always going through life 'sticking my neck out.'"

Throughout the course of her spiritual seeking, Esther came to realize the insights into one's own character and into the character of others that can be obtained by studying the hidden symbolism within totemism.

For example, she pointed out that the giraffe is associated with the cycle of power invested in farsightedness. Its elongated neck, legs, and body symbolize a bridge, a way to cross over into new realms and new perceptions. The giraffe is known for its keen eyesight. This and its magnificent height are powerful totems for seeing what lies over the horizon.

Esther also noted that while the giraffe does not have true antlers, it does have horns that are somewhat different from those found on other horned animals. It has also been noted that the giraffe has a "third horn," which is actually a lump under the skin located in the traditional position of the third eye, which in ancient teachings represents the seat of higher intuition.

"The slender, long legs of the giraffe symbolize the ability to maintain balance, yet to move and to progress," she said. "Those who cherish the giraffe as a totem animal are helped to keep their legs and feet on the ground, their head to the sky, and their eyes on the horizon. Communing with the giraffe totem can reveal the future and show how best to move beyond fear and a resistance to change and demonstrate how to accomplish this in a graceful, elegant fashion.

"I now realize that when I take my eyes off the horizon, lower my head, hunch my shoulders, and allow the strains of life to bend my back, I become more vulnerable to the vicissitudes of life," Esther observed. "Things don't go well when I allow my life to become static, and I become too satisfied with my past accomplishments. The secret is in the seeking."

Esther revealed that she received the gift of a second totem in late 1994. She could remember the exact day and moment:

"I was meditating—which I have done for forty years—in the backseat of a car on a trip across the Nevada/Idaho border. I 'saw' an animal that was unfamiliar to me. It was tawny and gray/white with pointed, tufted ears, big paws, and an innocent-appearing face. The word 'lynx' occurred to me along with the thought that this was my second power animal. I asked my husband what a lynx looked like, and he described a bobcat-like creature with tufted ears, short tail, and big paws."

Soon after receiving her new totem animal, she seemed to undergo a series of synchronistic happenings, all having to do with the lynx. These occurrences, she came to realize, were meant to teach her to be constantly aware of the hidden messages in everyday synchronicities.

"The lynx symbolizes the unseen and visions of the hidden," she said. "Thus, both of my totem animals brought me similar vibrations in this regard.

"The eyes of a newborn lynx are blue, but within ninety days, they turn yellow. To students of totemism, this symbolizes the drawing of knowledge from the heavens. My own eyes are hazel, a sort of yellowish brown-green.

"From the metaphysical standpoint, the lynx is associated with the number eleven, a master number indicative of inspiration, revelation, mysticism, hidden teachings, and the art of prescience. My life numbers are 3, 8, and 11."

Esther said that according to her studies, giraffe and lynx people are said to have the ability to see error and to sense when someone is lying to them. Such clairvoyant vision can make some sensitive individuals somewhat reluctant to be around those with these totem animals.

"People with these totem animals must learn to trust their instincts when it comes to associating with others," Esther advised. "They can be gullible and taken in by others if they choose to ignore their intuition."

In *Man, God and Magic*, ethnologist Ivar Lissner ponders the provocative mystery of why those anonymous Franco-Cantabrian cave artists of over 20,000 years ago never left us any clearly defined self-portraits that would depict the actual physical appearance of our ancestors. Aside from a few Venus-type mother-goddess statuettes, we are left with a strange collection of ghostly creatures and a great variety of two-legged beings with the heads of animals and birds. Thus, despite their remarkable artistic gifts, our ancestors never passed on an accurate idea of their features and confined themselves to portraying beings that were half-human, half-animal.

But then Lissner has an inspiration. It is possible, he suggests, that the Stone-Age artists really were portraying themselves, ". . . but in something more than human shape, in the guise of intermediary beings who were stronger than common men and able to penetrate more deeply into the mysteries of fate, that unfathomable interrelationship between animals, men, and gods."

What the ancient cave painters may have been telling us is that the ". . . road to supernatural powers is easier to follow in animal shape and that spirits can only be reached with an animal's assistance." The artists may have been portraying themselves after all, but in animal guise, ecstatically or shamanistically.

## Four Effortless Ways to Select Your Animal Totem

So your surname is not Bear, Bull, Crow, Fox, Hawk, Wolf or that of any other animal. How should you go about selecting the totem that will represent your spirit helper?

Perhaps, like Esther Hamel with her giraffe, you have had a lifelong attraction to one or more animals. You may have been collecting statues, paintings, or photographs of a particular creature without really having a clear mental picture of why you were so fascinated with this one special animal. On one level of consciousness, you may already have been aware of the identity of your animal totem.

## Attaining Your Animal Totem
## from Your Zodiacal Birth Sign

If your shelves are not stocked with objects of art representing frogs, eagles, cats, horses, elephants, or any other creature in particular, then perhaps the simplest method of acquiring a totem animal—other than being born with an animal surname—is to accept the symbol of your birth sign as your spirit helper.

Of course, those of you who know that your sign is Gemini, Virgo, Libra, Sagittarius, or Aquarius are already complaining that you have no animal representation. I was put on the spot about that once before in front of a seminar audience and spontaneously, without time for conscious cerebral activity, Spirit provided me with animals to fill those gaps. It is, of course, up to those who are born under those signs to accept or reject the totems revealed to me—but remember, you had none before.

If the animal designated as yours by virtue of your birth sign intrigues you but still leaves you a bit uncertain, check the Totem Animal Dictionary beginning on page 151 for additional information about that particular animal.

Aries, the Ram: March 21 to April 20
Taurus, the Bull: April 21 to May 21
Gemini, the Dolphin: May 22 to June 21
Cancer, the Crab: June 22 to July 22
Leo, the Lion: July 23 to August 23
Virgo, the Lamb: August 24 to September 22
Libra, the Owl: September 23 to October 23
Scorpio, the Scorpion: October 24 to November 22
Sagittarius, the Horse: November 23 to December 21
Capricorn, the Goat: December 22 to January 20
Aquarius, the Eagle: January 21 to February 19
Pisces, the Fish: February 20 to March 20

### The Native American Zodiac

If you don't feel connected on a spiritual level with the animal totem provided with your birth date in the standard zodiacal depictions (with my few modifications) try blending with your animal sign from the Native American Zodiac, based on the Medicine Wheel cosmology interpreted by my friends Wabun and the late Sun Bear:

> The Red-Tailed Hawk: March 19 to April 19
> The Beaver: April 20 to May 20
> The Deer: May 21 to June 21
> The Brown Flicker: June 22 to July 21
> The Sturgeon: July 22 to August 21
> The Bear: August 22 to September 22
> The Raven: September 23 to October 22
> The Snake: October 23 to November 21
> The Elk: November 22 to December 21
> The Snow Goose: December 22 to January 20
> The Otter: January 20 to February 18
> The Cougar: February 19 to March 20

### The Chinese Zodiac

Exponents of the Chinese Zodiac believe that the year of a person's birth is the primary factor in the determining of his or her personality traits, physical and mental attributes, and the degree of happiness and success attained throughout that person's lifetime. The Chinese Zodiac consists of a twelve-year cycle, each year of which is named after a different animal totem that imparts distinct characteristics to those born in a given year. If you have not yet found the totem animal that truly resonates with your inner self, perhaps you will be able to claim the animal sign of your birth year as your spirit helper. (If you were born before 1936, add twelve to the year you were born in to determine your year and sign.)

> The Rat: 1936, 1948, 1960, 1972, 1984, 1996
> The Ox: 1937, 1949, 1961, 1973, 1985, 1997

The Tiger: 1938, 1950, 1962, 1974, 1986, 1998
The Rabbit: 1939, 1951, 1963, 1975, 1987, 1999
The Dragon: 1940, 1952, 1964, 1976, 1988, 2000
The Snake: 1941, 1953, 1965, 1977, 1989, 2001
The Horse: 1942, 1954, 1966, 1978, 1990, 2002
The Sheep: 1943, 1955, 1967, 1979, 1991, 2003
The Monkey: 1944, 1956, 1968, 1980, 1992, 2004
The Cock: 1945, 1957, 1969, 1981, 1993, 2005
The Dog: 1946, 1958, 1970, 1982, 1994, 2006
The Boar: 1947, 1959, 1971, 1983, 1995, 2007

## ACCEPTING THE ANIMAL TOTEM OF YOUR PATRON SAINT

Many of the saints of Christendom are identified by an animal symbol. If you don't feel a rapport with the animal totem based on your zodiacal sign, perhaps you may decide that if a particular creature was good enough for your patron saint, it is good enough for you.

Bear: St. Gall
Bee: St. Ambrose, St. John Chrysostom
Birds: St. Francis of Assisi
Blackbird: St. Kevin
Boar: St. Cyricus
Bull: St. Luke, St. Thomas Aquinas
Camel: St. Mennas
Cock: St. Peter, St. Vitus
Cow: St. Brigid
Crow: St. Anthony
Doe: St. Withburga
Dog: St. Dominic, St. Hubert, St. Bernard
Dove: St. Ambrose, St. Gregory
Dragon: St. George, St. Margaret of Antioch
Eagle: St. John the Evangelist
Fish: St. Anthony of Padua
Goose: St. Brigid, St. Martin
Lamb: St. Agnes, St. John the Baptist
Lion: St. Mark, St. Jerome
Mouse: St. Gertrude of Nivelles

Otter: St. Cuthbert
Pig: St. Anthony of Egypt
Salmon: St. Kentigern
Snake: St. Patrick
Stag: St. Eustace, St. Giles
Swan: St. Hugh of Lincoln
Whale: St. Brendan
Wolf: St. Edmund of East Anglia, St. Francis of Assisi

## RECEIVING YOUR TOTEM DURING A SIMULATED VISION QUEST

Here is a guided visualization that I have used with great success at
seminars throughout the United States and Canada. The goal of the
exercise is to simulate a traditional Native American vision quest and
enable the participants to receive their spirit helper, or animal totem.

You will need a time and a place in which you are certain to be
undisturbed for at least half an hour. This exercise requires you to be
in as relaxed a state as possible in order to receive suggestions and to
act upon them with maximum effect. For that purpose, I am providing a relaxation process that you will be able to use for each of the
guided visualizations in this book.

You may wish to have a family member or friend read the relaxation process and the guided visualization to you in a soft, soothing
voice. I have found the use of Native American flute music softly
playing in the background to be a most effective aid in achieving ex-
ceptional results with this exercise. If you do use music as background, be certain that it does not contain any lyrics, for they are
likely to distract you from attaining full benefit from the technique.

Some people have told me that they like to record the relaxation
process and the guided visualization using their own voice to guide
them through the vision quest. Either method can be effective, and
your success truly depends upon your willingness to visualize in your
mind the conditions of your vision quest.

Assume a comfortable position, either sitting or lying down, that
you can maintain for thirty minutes. Take a comfortably deep breath
. . . and being to relax.

## THE RELAXATION PROCESS

Visualize that at your feet there lies a soft, warm, rose-colored blanket. It has been learned that the color rose stimulates natural body warmth and helps to induce sleep and relaxation. It also provides a sense of well-being and a great feeling of being loved.

Imagine that you are mentally moving the rose-colored blanket slowly up over your body. Feel it moving over your feet, relaxing them. Feel it moving over your legs, relaxing them. Feel it moving over your stomach, removing all tensions . . . over your back, removing all stress.

With every breath that you take, you find that you are becoming more and more relaxed. With every breath that you take, you find that you are becoming more and more peaceful.

Any sound that you might hear—a barking dog, a slamming door, a honking car horn—will not disturb you. Any sound that you hear will only help you to relax . . . relax . . . relax.

Now you are mentally pulling the rose-colored blanket over your chest, your arms, relaxing them . . . relaxing them. As the blanket moves over your neck, relaxing all the muscles of your neck, visualize the rose-colored blanket transforming itself into a hood that covers your head like a cowl. Now you are completely enveloped in the beautiful rose-colored blanket, and you feel the color of rose permeating your psyche, permitting you to relax . . . relax . . . relax.

Now imagine that there lies at your feet a soft, warm blanket the color of green. Green is a cleanser, a healer, that will help you to relax even deeper. Visualize yourself pulling the green blanket slowly over your body.

Feel it moving over your feet, relaxing them, healing them of any pain. Feel the lovely green blanket moving over your legs, relaxing them, healing them of any discomfort. Feel it moving over your stomach, ridding it of all tensions. Feel it moving over your chest, your arms . . . relaxing, healing, relaxing.

With every breath that you take, you are becoming more and more relaxed . . . more at peace . . . more and more at one with your body, mind, and spirit.

Feel the healing color of green moving over your back, relaxing all the stress along the spine. Feel the color of green relaxing, healing, relaxing your entire body.

As you make a hood of the green blanket, pull it over your head, calming all of your nerves, your anxieties, your stresses. You are now completely enveloped in the healing color of green, and you feel it permeate your psyche, relaxing you . . . calming you . . . healing you.

Visualize now a gold blanket at your feet. The color of gold has long been recognized as a great strengthener of the nervous system. Imagine now that you are slowly pulling the soft, warm, beautiful gold blanket over your body.

Feel it moving over your feet, calming you, relaxing you. Feel it moving over your legs, calming you, relaxing you. Feel it moving slowly over your stomach, soothing any nervous condition, healing any pain. Feel the lovely gold blanket moving slowly over your chest, your arms, your back, soothing you, relaxing you.

Nothing will disturb you, nothing will distress you. All concerns are being left behind . . . as you become more and more relaxed . . . relaxed . . . relaxed.

Feel the gold blanket fashioning itself into a protective hood that covers your head and completely bathes you in the color of gold. Feel the color of gold permeating your brain, your nervous system, permitting your body-mind-spirit network to create a healthier, happier you. Relax . . . relax . . . as you prepare to receive a teaching vision from the Great Mystery.

Visualize now at your feet a blanket the color of blue. Blue prompts psychic sensitivity. The color of blue will aid you greatly in receiving dream or vision teachings of a positive and helpful nature.

Imagine now that you are willing the blue-colored blanket to move slowly up your body. Feel it moving slowly over your feet, relaxing them. Feel it moving over your legs, your hips, re-laxing them . . . relaxing them.

With every breath you take, you are becoming more and more relaxed . . . more and more prepared to be at one with the Great Mystery . . . more and more at peace.

Now feel the blue blanket moving slowly over your chest, your arms, your back, your stomach, removing all tensions, all stresses. Everywhere the blue blanket touches you, you feel a wonderful relaxing energy moving throughout every cell of your body. Everywhere the blue blanket touches you, you feel re-laxed . . . relaxed . . . relaxed.

As the blue blanket becomes a beautiful blue cowl, imagine that the color of blue is about to permeate your psyche and give you the wisdom to receive profound teachings from the Great Mystery. Know that the color of blue will accelerate all your psychic abilities.

Now bring the beautiful blue cowl over your head and allow it to envelope you completely in its peaceful, relaxing, loving energy.

## THE VISION QUEST EXERCISE

See yourself now as a Native American man or woman on a vi-sion quest. You know that you have the ability to draw power and strength from the Great Mystery and to receive your true spirit helper, your animal totem. You know that you have the ability to evolve as a spiritual being on your lifepath on the Earth Mother.

Focus now on the performance of some mundane, monoto-nous physical task to exhaust the body and tire the mind. See that you stand in a small clearing in the forest which has a number of rocks of various sizes at one end of the barren area. Pick up one of the rocks and carry it to the opposite side of the clearing. See yourself carrying the rock. Feel the rough surface of the rock on your hands. Feel the weight of it pull at your arm muscles.

See yourself placing the rock down on the ground and turning around to get another rock. See yourself picking up a new rock and carrying it slowly to the other side of the clearing . . . and then another rock . . . and another . . . back and forth . . . back and forth . . . over and over again.

Know and understand that you are performing this task for the sole purpose of depleting the physical self with monotonous exercise. Know and understand that you are distracting the conscious mind with dull activity, so that your spirit can soar to the Great Mystery.

Feel now your body becoming very tired . . . very heavy. You have no aching muscles or sore tendons, but you are very, very tired. See yourself lying down on a blanket to relax . . . relax . . . relax.

Slowly you become aware of a presence. Someone has approached you and has come to stand next to you. You feel no fear. You feel only peace and love.

As you look up from your blanket, you see two Grandparents who have come from the spirit world to look at you on your quest. You see that they are majestic in appearance. They smile at you . . . then disappear.

Your inner knowing tells you that they came to you to show you that in many ways, on many levels, you have a great partnership with the world of spirits. The Grandparents have given you a sign of the reality of your oneness with all spiritual beings.

You have but a moment to ponder the wonder of the spirit visitation when you become aware of a globe of bluish white light moving toward you. You are not afraid, for you sense a great spiritual presence approaching you.

As the light swirls and becomes solid, you behold before you a man or a woman in spirit whom you regard as a saint, a great Medicine Chief, a master, an illumined one. This figure, so beloved to you, gestures to your left side. As you turn, you are astonished to behold a marvelous link-up with other holy figures from all times, all places, all cultures. You see that these great spiritual beings form a chain of Spirit from prehistory to the present and into the future.

The sacred one before you smiles benevolently, then bends over and gently touches your eyes, your ears, and your mouth. You know within that this holy touching symbolizes that you must share your revelations with others.

As the holy one begins to fade from your perception, you now perceive a brilliant white light so bright that you must cover your eyes. You feel no fear, only love emanating from the bright light. Your inner knowing makes you aware that within this powerful light is your spirit helper, whose identity will soon be made known to you in physical form.

Now, in a great rush of color and light, you are made aware that you are being elevated in spirit. You know that your spirit helper has taken you to a higher vibrational level. You have moved to a dimension where nonlinear, cyclical time flows around you. The energy of the Great Mystery touches you, and you are made aware that you are becoming one with the great pattern of all life.

You see before you now an animal, any animal that enters into your consciousness. Become one with its essence. Become one with this level of awareness. Be that animal. Be that level of energy expression.

See before you now a bird, any bird that enters into your consciousness. Become one with its essence. Become one with its level of awareness. Be that bird. Be that level of energy expression.

See before you now a creature of the waters, any creature of the waters that enters your consciousness. Become one with its essence. Become one with its level of awareness. Be that creature of the waters. Be that level of energy expression.

See before you now a creeper or a crawler, any creeper or crawler that enters your consciousness. Become one with its essence. Become one with its level of awareness. Be that creeper or crawler. Be that level of energy expression.

See before you now an insect, any insect that enters your consciousness. Become one with its essence. Become one with its level of awareness. Be that insect. Be that level of energy expression.

See before you now a plant, any plant that enters your consciousness. Become one with its essence. Become one with its level of awareness. Be that plant. Be that level of energy expression.

Know that you are now one with the unity of all plant and animal essence.

Know now that you are one with all things that walk on two legs or four, with all things that fly, with all things that crawl, with all things that sustain themselves in the waters, with all things that grow in the soil.

And now your spirit helper will show you the image of your animal totem.

At the count of three, you will focus upon that creature. You will see its beauty. You will become one with its beauty. At the count of three, you will know that this animal is now your totem, the symbol that will often come to you in dreams and represent your spirit helper on another level of reality.

One . . . the image is beginning to appear before you.

Two . . . you are beginning to see clearly the image of your animal totem, your spirit helper.

Three . . . you see clearly the image of your animal totem!

At this eternal second in the energy of the Eternal Now, at this vibrational level of oneness with all living things, at this frequency of awareness of unity with the cosmos, your animal totem is permitting you to receive a great teaching vision of something about which you need to know for your good and your gaining.

Receive this great vision now! (*Allow approximately two minutes to pass before speaking again.*)

You will return to full consciousness at the count of five. You will be filled with positive memories of your vision quest. You are now fully aware of the identity of your animal totem, your spirit helper. You will awaken feeling better and healthier than ever before in your life, and you will feel a great sense of unity with all living things.

One . . . coming awake. Two . . . more and more awake. Three . . . feeling very good in mind, body, and spirit. Four . . .

coming wide awake now. Five . . . wide awake and feeling wonderful!

### "WE CAN UTILIZE ANIMAL TEACHINGS IN EVERYTHING WE DO"

Julia White's workshops in Native American Awareness include sessions in which she helps her students learn how to use their animal totems to improve their lives.

"It is time again to learn and practice the teachings of the animals," Julia said recently. "We are once again becoming increasingly aware of the value of animals and the teachings that they have always had for us.

"In the beginning, when humankind was new to the earth, it was the animals who allowed us to survive. As we became 'civilized,' we began to lose our respect for the animal kingdom that had sustained us. At last, the pendulum is beginning its swing back to esteem for the animals so that we strive to preserve and protect them."

"I am the Wolf," she says. "I must teach. I want to bring people to a greater awareness of all things and empower them to have courage and to live without fear."

Teaching has always been in Julia's blood, ever since she was in second grade helping the first-graders learn how to read. Later, she taught personal law, business administration, and office skills at the junior college level for ten years. Today, operating out of Long Beach, California, she helps men and women find their own paths to awareness.

Julia's grandfather was a tall, fair-skinned, blue-eyed blond German from North Carolina, who had met and married a full-blooded Catawba. "When you looked into grandmother's face, you knew that she carried the wisdom of the ages and that she could see forever," Julia remembers.

At that time in the deep South it was against the law for a White to marry a Native American or anyone of color, so her grandparents bought a fairly large parcel of land along the banks of the Catawba River and settled down to raise their family in peace. Julia's father was a full-blooded Cherokee who was killed working on the railroad as a wrecking engineer when she was a child of four.

"So there I was," Julia recalled, "one-fourth German, one-fourth Catawba, and one-half Cherokee—a fatherless, blue-eyed, blond outcast. I was given my grandmother's name, Julia, and I remember that she would call me her 'little Indian.'"

From the day she entered this earthwalk, Julia said, she has had the silver wolf on her left, protecting her feminine side, and the otter on her right, protecting her masculine side—clearly reversed for balance. "Everything that I am and have been throughout my life has reflected these two energies, even long before I knew what a totem animal is. I simply walk their paths—and don't know how not to. I am they, and they are me. I don't do anything to 'call them up,' for they never leave me."

Julia describes how, by having them tell her their favorite animal, she successfully gets her students to understand how we all reflect animal teachings:

I explain the message of that animal. Then we explore the animals they fear or hate, and why. Next, I have each person make a list of the personality traits they dislike the most in themselves (the beginning of insight, honesty, and self-examination), as well as the things about themselves that they really do like. I go over the lists, find the behaviors that appear most often in each list, and then we discuss them and the animals that carry those teachings.

By now the students are beginning to get two things: We are animals and we share certain common traits. We take the "bad" habits and choose the animal with the teaching that is the opposite.

I asked Julia how she determines a totem animal for one's feminine and masculine sides.

"It is usually not up to us to make the choice," she replied, "at least not for those of us who are spiritually and metaphysically aware. We know by instinct because we 'feel' them. If the situation should be to help someone keep a good balance in his or her outlook on life, the male energy animal will be on the left, and vice versa.

"If we are out of balance—too opinionated, too aggressive, too set in our ways, too dependent, and so forth—then we should seek out an animal with the opposite teachings and carry it with us on the side of the body that needs the support. We can carry a feather, a claw, a piece of fur, a tooth, whatever we can."

I wondered how she advised her students to use their totem animals in the process of creative dreaming.

"I suggest that they ask the dominant and permanent animal from either the right side or the left side to take them into the dream state. For example, soar on the eagle's back, ride the bear, walk with the deer, swim with the dolphin. That totem animal will usually lead them to the animal who is the keeper of the insight that they seek, and they will journey together."

Julia insists that we can utilize animal teachings in everything that we do by learning the message that each creature has for us.

"From the bird family we learn to ride the winds of change," she begins, listing her examples. "We learn to live in the moment and to act accordingly, for a bird who hesitates when his lunch passes by will go hungry.

"Parrots teach us the art of communication skills," she continued. "Crows teach us about fair trade and barter. The birds of prey are living examples of maintaining a broad overview of life so that we don't develop tunnel vision. The hummingbird carries a message of adaptability, making the most of every situation.

"Deer reflect a quiet determination to accomplish each task with gentleness. The Elk tell us that people can work well together with their own kind without merciless competition. The big predator cats carry the strength of independence and the power of the family unit."

And wherever we are, whatever we are doing, Julia states, we can carry reminders with us of our animal teachers.

"It's easy to carry a small picture of a fox with us to remind us of the value of silence," she said. "A small picture of a dolphin prompts us to use our breath to relieve stress and to move with the ebb and flow of life. Do you know someone who is a sourpuss? Give him a picture of a coyote leaping into the air.

"Learn about animal teachings," Julia White concludes. "Watch their behavior. Use their wisdom for a more alert, aware, and rewarding life."

## Match Your Lifepath Number with that of Your Totem

Another method of discovering your animal totem—or of evaluating a totem's potential strengths to balance with your own abilities—is to utilize the ancient science of numerology to determine the number of your lifepath and the soul urge number of your spirit helper. For centuries now, certain metaphysicians have been claiming that the totality of human experience on the earthwalk can be reduced to the digits 1 through 9—with the exception of the master numbers 1 and 22, which are not broken down. By learning how to analyze one's numerical makeup, these individuals maintain, it is possible to determine one's potential, hidden aptitudes, talents, and desires.

For example, my lifepath number is 4, which means that I am a good organizer who seeks to build things of lasting importance. When I add the soul urge numbers, the inner strengths, of my totem animals, I gain adaptability from Wolf, who is a 2; wisdom from Crow, who adds a 7; and universality and humanitarianism from Dog, who brings us a 9. If I want to assess my numerological linkup with my spirit helpers even further, I can add my own soul urge number of 11 to the mix, which adds the element of the visionary and the dreamer. All in all, then, I must say that I am pleased with the story that the numbers tell me about the interaction between my psyche and my animal totems and the balance that they bring to my life.

Here is how I determined my lifepath number. Using my birthdate of February 19, 1936, we note that February is the second month, which gives us a 2. The day 1 + 9 = 10, which reduces to 1 because the zero is not counted. Add the month and the day together and I have a 3. The year—1 + 9 + 3 + 6 = 19, which reduces to a 1. Add 3 + 1 and I have 4, the number of my lifepath.

To determine the number power of your name or that of your totem's, use the following graph:

| 1 | 2 | 3 | 4 | 5 | 6 | 7 | 8 | 9 |
|---|---|---|---|---|---|---|---|---|
| A | B | C | D | E | F | G | H | I |
| J | K | L | M | N | O | P | Q | R |
| S | T | U | V | W | X | Y | Z |   |

Examples:

| W | O | L | F | |
|---|---|---|---|---|
| 5 | +6 | +3 | +6 | = 20 = 2 |

| B | R | A | D | S | T | E | I | G | E | R |
|---|---|---|---|---|---|---|---|---|---|---|
| 2 | 9 | 1 | 4 | 1 | 2 | 5 | 9 | 7 | 5 | 9 |
| | | | 16 | | | | 31 | | | |
| | | | 7 | | | | 4 = 11 | | | |

Here is a brief description of the meaning of each of the numbers one to nine and the master numbers, eleven and twenty-two. Study the numbers of your totem animals and your own name and lifepath to gain additional insight into the various strengths and weaknesses of your spiritual team. Then strive for balance and harmony.

1. Key word: *Individualization*. Negative vibrational pole: *Self-Centered*. Number One personalities are independent beings who feel the need to use their own powers and their own brains to devise original methods of doing things. They are compelled to be creative, and they control body, mind, and spirit to the utmost efficiency. Those who bear this number on their lifepath accept no limitations, yet they must learn the balance of cooperation without the loss of individuality.

2. Key word: *Adaptability*. Negative vibrational pole: *Self-Effacement*. Number Two personalities are excellent diplomats and peacemakers. They are attracted to groups and to communities; and they make excellent spouses, for they enjoy serving others with love and consideration. They are good mixers and are sensitive to rhythm and music.

3. Key word: *Self-Expression*. Negative vibrational pole: *Superficiality*. Those who walk this lifepath are individuals who have discovered the joy of living. They tend to find their opportunities in circulating and socializing and are generally considered the "life of the party." An artistic environment is best for Number Three personalities, for they are always seeking expression through writing, painting, speaking, or music.

4. Key word: *Organization*. Negative vibrational pole: *Hypercritical*. Number Four personalities are the builders, those who begin with a firm foundation and construct something of lasting importance. They serve patiently and dependably and are capable of great achievements. Four is the number of Mother Earth, and so are Number Four beings down-to-earth. They do the job at hand, striving always to perfect the form of the task before them.

5. Key word: *Freedom*. Negative vibrational pole: *Self-Indulgence*. Number Five types must be prepared for frequent and unexpected change and variety. Because Five personalities do a great deal of traveling, they learn to understand all classes and conditions of the Earth Mother's creatures. Number Five beings are always seeking the new and progressive. Interestingly, the lifepath of the United States is a five.

6. Key word: *Adjustment*. Negative vibrational pole: *Tyranny*. Number Six personalities are the responsible ones, because six is the number of devotional, impersonal love. Those who bear this number on their lifepath serve quietly, cheerfully, and efficiently, applying the law of balance to adjust inharmonious conditions. Others often come to them for material and spiritual aid, and they are always willing to give it.

7. Key word: *Wisdom*. Negative vibrational pole: *Withdrawal*. Seven is a cosmic number vibrationally related to the seven days of the week, seven notes of the musical scale, seven colors in the rainbow, and so forth. Opportunities come to Seven personalities without their actively seeking them. Those who bear this number are determined to seek answers to the deep mysteries and hidden truths of the universe. They are unconcerned with material goods, for these potential mystics know that by applying spiritual laws, they will prosper.

8. Key word: *Material Freedom*. Negative vibrational pole: *Demander*. Those who resonate with this number in their earthwalk are the practical beings of the material world, and they usually achieve love, power, and success. Number Eight personalities are willing to work and are prepared to take any opportunity to demonstrate their effi-

ciency. Eight is a power number. Like electricity, it has the energy to bring light—or to electrocute.

9. Key word: *Universality*. Negative vibrational pole: *Egocentricity*. This is the number that represents the Oneness of all living things. This is a difficult path, for it requires the complete expression of unconditional love. Number Nine personalities must be prepared to give up all personal desire and ambition. They will find their greatest opportunities in the spheres of the emotional, artistic, and inspirational. Number Nine operates under the Law of Fulfillment, and its appeal is to the all-inclusive, the many.

11. A Master Number. Key word: *Revelation*. Negative vibrational pole: *Fanaticism*. Number Eleven personalities are the dreamers, the visionaries, those who receive their ideals intuitively. Those on this vibration are on a higher plane than that of the strictly material, and their destiny is to reveal something new and uplifting to the world. Those who bear the master number Eleven on their earthwalk are the messengers, the spokespeople, the broadcasters.

22. A Master Number. Key word: *Material Master*. Negative vibrational pole: *Self-Promoter*. Those who represent the master number Twenty-Two on their lifepath are the pragmatic idealists who take the dreams of Number Eleven and put them to practical use. Number Twenty-two personalities are concerned with the progress of humankind. They readily conceive philanthropic projects and plans, and they work steadily for the improvement and welfare of the masses.

## "YOUR TOTEM ANIMAL WILL TELL YOU WHAT YOU NEED TO KNOW"

Tara Buckland of Wooster, Ohio, tells me that as she looks back over the years, it is easy to see that from the time she was a very small child, Snake, her totem animal, has always been there protecting her.

"In those early years, I had several peaceful snake encounters that left deep impressions," she says, "but it was not until 1989, just after the Chinese New Year ushered in the Year of the Snake, that Snake made her presence known to me in a conscious way."

A new girlfriend invited Tara over to her house, and there, in the living room, was a gigantic glass cage filled with a six-and-a-half-foot-long red-tailed boa constrictor. Tara felt her heart "skip a few beats and begin to race." She was thrilled and frightened at the same time.

Her friend offered to let Tara hold the huge snake.

"There was no hesitation," she recalls. "I had to touch her. She was quite heavy, and when she lifted her head to look in my eyes, I felt a deep jolt that pierced my soul. There was also a sense of recognition."

At first Tara's only thought was to acquire a "pet" snake, which she did. "But then it became so much more. I learned about totems and began to suspect that my snake friends were far more than 'pets.'

"Once Snake entered my life, so many changes began. Good changes like suddenly being able to buy my first house—but also deep changes began. The early stages of a mid-life crisis had evoked questions such as: Who am I? Where am I going? Is this all there is to life? What about all those adolescent dreams of greatness? Snake seemed to usher in a shakedown. I needed to shed my skin."

Tara's girlfriend must have known what was happening to her, for one day she came by Tara's place and told her that she had brought a present for her.

"She looked deeply into my eyes and presented me with a lovely copper snake bracelet. She said that it had been given to her long ago, but now I must have it. As she slipped it on my wrist, the hairs on my arms stood up. It felt as though I had undergone some sort of initiation. Since then I have bought many beautiful pieces of snake jewelry, but that simple copper bracelet remains my favorite."

After her "initiation," Tara says that she expended a great deal of energy into learning all that she could about snakes. She acquired several snakes and even trained the largest one, a Northern Pine, to go "potty" in a particular designated spot in the house.

But Snake told Tara that she had much more to learn, and she was directed to research snake-related mythology.

"I was not permitted to get too involved in any one culture or perspective. Snake insisted I take it all in—and the amount of information was staggering."

After a lengthy period of study, Tara began to wonder how to apply such wide-ranging knowledge in her own life.

"I didn't have long to wonder, for Snake has always been very exacting with what She wants. Snake can be many things to many people, but to me the word 'totem' best fits. As a totem, She becomes a conduit or channel to my Higher Self. My Higher Self links me to God/Goddess/All-That-Is. That's a roundabout way of saying that the visual symbol of a Snake puts me in touch with the Divine. I have no idea how or why this works, but I see it as a special gift with which a totem can bless a person.

"Snake opens doors to the unconscious, protects my sacred space, and gives me insight and help when things get tough. So I pray to Snake. Sounds old-fashioned and a bit blasphemous to my Presbyterian upbringing, but that's about what it boils down to. Of course, Snake is not the only Being I pray to, but I always remember Her in my prayers."

Tara explains that Snake talks to her most often through dreams. Although she had never experienced a snake dream in her life until her "initiation" in 1989, it is now unusual to go for more than a week or so without a dream appearance of Snake.

Certain mythologies claim that all snakes are healers. While Tara does not claim experience with "all" snakes, she does have one modest red Corn snake named Maizey that she considers her healing snake.

"It happened quite by accident that I began noticing that Maizey could heal people. A friend was holding her when Maizey crawled around to her back and decided to take a snooze. Twenty minutes later when my friend had to leave and handed Maizey back to me, she noticed that her backache had disappeared. After a few more episodes like this, friends began asking to hold Maizey. She never seemed to mind, and she would always crawl on her own accord to the hurtful spot and then go into trance. When the healing was completed, she would just crawl off the 'patient' and slip down the back of the sofa."

Tara also uses Snake as a messenger whenever she needs to do long-distance healing.

"For example, once I sent a few rainbow-colored snakes on the astral level to a friend who was ill. She didn't like snakes, so I didn't tell her what I was doing. I just told her that I would pray for her. The next day she called to tell me that she had had this weird dream about snakes. And even though she was afraid of snakes, she said that these snakes weren't 'scary.' She knew that as they encircled her they were giving her healing and protective energy."

Although Tara doesn't feel the need to engage in a great deal of ritual for Snake, there are a few things that she does to "feed" the Spirit.

"First and foremost is dancing and drumming. Pounding away on my hand-drums really seems to get my totem jumping. I usually reach a point where I can't drum any more. Then I just have to jump up and dance and express myself. Snake always comes through very strongly then.

"Drums awaken Kundalini, the Inner Serpent Fire that starts as a rumbling deep in my bowels and builds in intensity until it shoots up my spine. At that point I might cry, laugh, get goosebumps, and so forth. It's a wonderful high, and I always get the feeling that Snake likes it when I dance for Her—or should I say with Her?"

Tara says that she had tried for several years to compose suitable prayers and chants for Snake, but she had always failed miserably.

"Snake finally revealed the problem. Snakes just don't go in much for language. Think about it. They don't whine, moan, bark, meow, growl, or yip. Since I love to talk, this has been a difficult lesson for me. Any communicating that I do with Snake is nonverbal. Sometimes even words that are thought are not useful.

"I have learned to communicate with nonthought. Practitioners of Zen recognize this as emptying the mind of conversations and thoughts. If there is something I wish to communicate or learn, it's best to express the thought, then let it go and attain emptiness. When I feel the desire to do something formal for Snake, it is usually a simple ritualistic use of rattle and dance. Occasionally I hiss."

In the spring, when snakes come out of winter hibernation, Tara throws a "welcome back" party for them to celebrate her totem. She even has the bakery make a cake with a snake decoration on it.

"I invite all my snake friends over and the evening is great. The highlight is when we all start to drum and stamp on the ground with the intention of awakening any sleepyheads. We light candles, feast, and sing. I have the strong feeling that Snake is able to receive the energy, and I know that she is well pleased."

Tara has observed that Snake seems interested in bringing together those who share her totem.

"I have met a fair number of people who have Snake as their totem, and we always form an instant bond. The really interesting thing is that when we compare notes, we find wonderful similarities of experience. This has enabled me to receive verification of the messages that I have been receiving. For example, many of us have had the exact same vision of a gigantic, black, iridescent Snake that dwells in the universe. We call Her Cosmic Grandmother Serpent."

Tara has also found it interesting to discover the importance of color to Snake. "We Snake People found that after Snake had come into our lives, we all developed a craving for vibrant colors. We all went out and bought bright clothes and outlandish hats."

For Tara Buckland, having a totem has been a wonderful experience. She does have more than one totem animal, but they are not as strong or as central to her spirit as is Snake.

"I tell Snake that I love her every day, and I see a glimmer of Her presence in the eyes of my beautiful pet snakes. If there is one thing that I want to pass on to others, it is this: Your totem will tell you exactly what you need to know. Just be patient."

# CHAPTER 3

# Entering Shamanic Time

**T**HOSE TOTEM ANIMALS who would guide us to the mysterious, transcendent reality beyond our material world stand at the portal of the Great Mystery that leads us to another dimension of time and space.

It is through that very portal that shamans must pass to gain their visions. And those of us who seek to enrich our lives through the transformative power of our spirit helpers must also travel the nonphysical pathway that takes us into the dimension in which visions live.

**41**

One of the most crucial elements in the practice of shamanism and in the effective use of our animal totems is the ability to rise above linear time. Whenever we work with Spirit we soon discover that the conventional concept of time existing in some sort of sequential stream flowing along in one dimension from Point A to Point Z is totally inadequate to provide us with a full assessment of reality. Clocks and watches and time zones are convenient for us when we are functioning in the ordinary, conscious, waking state, but when we seek transcendence, we must rise to a level of awareness wherein past, present, and future form an Eternal Now. We gain access to this level of consciousness in our dreams and in our visions.

Mystics, Shamans, Medicine practitioners, and traditional people in general function extremely well in a nonlinear time construct. In his text for Ira Moskowitz's book of drawings, *American Indian Ceremonial Dances,* John Collier reflects upon the traditional Native American's possession of a time sense that was different—and happier—than the White man's:

> Once our white race had it, too, and then the mechanized world took it away from us. . . . We think, now, that any other time than linear, chronological time is an escapist dream. The Indians tell us otherwise, and their message and demonstration addresses itself to one of our deepest distresses and most forlorn yearnings. . . .
>
> . . . Did there exist—as the Indians in their whole life affirm—a dimension of time—a reality of time—not linear, not clock-measured, clock-controlled, and clock-ended for us, we would be glad; we would enter it and expand our being there. . . .
>
> In solitary, mystical experience many of ourselves do enter another time dimension. But under the frown of clockwork time which claims the world, we place our experience out in an eternity beyond the years and beyond the stars.

When you are given a vision teaching by your spirit helper, you are taken out of your body and lifted away from the physical dimensions of the Earth Mother. You feel more alive, more complete, more a part of the Oneness of the Great Mystery. You feel freer than you have ever felt before, and you know that the energy from your animal totem, your spirit helper, is guiding, guarding, and protecting you.

One of your greatest assets in achieving empowerment from your animal totem will be your ability to enter altered states of consciousness through meditation—going into the Silence—or through such exercises as I have included in this book. The receiving of a teaching vision comes when your mind is quiet, when you have entered the Silence and gone deep within.

When you enter the Silence, you must listen, wait, and prepare to receive. Remember that prayer is not meditation. Prayer is speaking, asking. Entering the Silence of deep meditation is an art form wherein you quietly receive the creative energy awaiting you.

## Gaining Sacred Power and Wisdom from Spirit Helpers

I want you to join me in a special experience. If you like, you may visualize it happening in a dream or a vision. Imagine that we are supplicants walking side by side as we approach the traditional Medicine lodge of a revered and powerful Shaman. We have made a long and arduous journey to sit at the feet of this highly esteemed practitioner of sacred magic. We have come to ask for guidance in achieving sacred power and wisdom through the use of our animal totems. As a gift for the Shaman we have brought tobacco or sweet grass, whichever you prefer.

Although this wise Shaman will speak of a number of Native American animal totems and tribal belief structures, this accomplished practitioner will also draw upon a wide range of shamanic traditions that have been acquired during his pilgrimages around the world. There is no question that we have come to the quintessential sacred teacher who will greatly expand our knowledge of how best to employ our spirit helpers. Before we enter the Medicine lodge, I want you to be aware that you may visualize the Shaman as either male or female, whichever you prefer or with whichever your inner guidance feels more comfortable.

Now imagine that a rather stern-faced elder opens the flap of the darkened lodge and indicates that we are now permitted to advance and to sit before the Shaman's fire. The smell of sage is heavy in the air. The Shaman shakes a rattle as we approach, and the elder motions that we should stand still before the Shaman while he fans the smoke of the burning sage over us with a hawk wing and asks a blessing of the four directions.

As we take positions before the mound of buffalo robes on which our sacred teacher sits, the ancient wise one begins our session by observing the age-old tradition of presenting credentials of shamanic accomplishment.

The Shaman speaks:

It is proper that you should know things about me and to learn of my ways. You will want to know about my medicine and my magic, and you will wish to hear of the wondrous deeds that I have accomplished among the humans and animals on earth and during my journeys in the spirit worlds.

This is not my first time to walk upon the Earth Mother. I have lived many times before. The first time was long, long ago when the great cave bears and the long-toothed lions made each night a time of terror. I was in a female body, and I served as an apprentice to our clan's Shaman. Together we made magic to keep our people safe from the great four-leggeds.

In the next life that I remember, I was a great warrior chief. I was killed in battle when I stumbled and a strong enemy split open my skull with a war club. At first I did not know that I was dead. It seemed that I awakened from the blow to my head and the battle was over. I got up and began to walk home to our village. I couldn't understand why none of the people of my village returned my salute. When I got to my home, my own children ignored me. They were clutching their mother's legs and crying. I spoke to my wife, but she did not seem to hear me. She, too, was weeping.

I stood there for a time, wondering what the matter could be. And then my spirit helper, the deer, appeared beside me, and I could hear his thoughts telling me that I was no longer in my body. I was now a spirit.

At first I could not believe this, for I felt no different. I felt strong and full of life. But my spirit helper told me to follow him, and he led me back to the place where my body had lain. Around me I could now see the spirit form of other warriors that had fallen that day. They, too, were walking with their spirit helpers. "Ho," I said to my guide, "it was a good day to die."

I thought that I would now go to our original home in the stars with the Grandparents, but I could not seem to do so. It seemed that I lingered near the battlefield for many winters.

At last my spirit helper came to me with a Shining One who explained to me that the Great Mystery had decreed that I should one day be a great Shaman. Therefore, my spirit must stay longer with the Earth Mother, and I must learn more about the four-leggeds, the winged ones, the water beings, and the crawlers. The Shining One told me that I must experience many different expressions of the Great Mystery, so that one day, when I was once again a human, I would be able to better serve my people as a great and powerful shaman. It would yet be many, many winters before I could return to the Oneness in the stars.

My spirit lived for a time in the body of a raven. It is a most wonderful existence to be able to fly, to soar high above the trees. To live as a raven was a great expression of freedom. Sometimes it felt as though I were a spirit again, rather than a living thing.

I must tell you, though, that the life of a raven was not as pleasant when snow and ice blanketed the Earth Mother. Food became very scarce. Sometimes I would swoop into a village and steal a scrap from the meat racks, but that was very dangerous.

Next, my spirit entered the body of a fish. I did not think this life was nearly as pleasant as being a raven. There was so little to do, except swim in the river and eat. Yet, the fish seemed so happy, and they danced in little circles with one another throughout most of every day.

When my spirit entered the body of a bear, I would often stand on my hind legs and walk as if I were again a human being. It felt good to be able to frighten both humans and animals. I understood why the bear has such powerful Medicine. He has great strength, but he does not abuse his power. He hunts only for the food he and his family needs, and he doesn't attack others unless greatly provoked.

After I had been a bear, my spirit lived for a time as a rattlesnake, a turtle, and a buffalo before the Shining One appeared and told me that I could now return to our original spirit home that exists far up above. This is the place from whence all spirits come to the Earth Mother.

When I first returned to the spirit home, I felt great honor. I met many Grandfathers and Grandmothers, and I learned much wisdom from many powerful Shamans and Magicians. But after I had been there for a time, I became lonesome for the places and the creatures that dwelt upon the Earth Mother. I went to a wise Medicine Doctor and told him that I wished to return to the green forests and the blue waters of Turtle Island.

The Medicine Doctor was not receptive to my words. He told me that I must first learn the power of breath. I must learn to control the *wakan*, the *orenda*, the *mana*, the sacred force that makes all Medicine and Magic work. To accomplish this great lesson, he told me that I must learn to play the flute and that I should not return to him until I had accomplished this task.

I think it must have been at least two earth years before I called again on the Medicine Doctor and played a beautiful melody for him on my flute. He agreed that I could now charm all spirits with my flute, but he now said that I must fast for twenty days before I came again to his lodge.

I did as he bade me, and when I returned weak and faint, the Medicine Doctor was sitting in his lodge surrounded by many spirits. At his feet there lay a large spirit cougar that snarled at me.

"The Spirit Council has agreed," the great Medicine Doctor said. "You may return to earth if you are able to defeat this mighty cat in combat."

The great cougar opened wide its mouth and stretched its enormous body to its full length. Its teeth were long and sharp. It held up a massive paw and showed me its terrible claws.

My only weapon was my flute, but I put it to my lips and I began to play the melody of a song that I had often heard the Grandmothers and Grandfathers singing in the spirit home. There was a bright flash of light, and the great cougar lay dead at my feet, with green blood oozing from its jaws.

The Medicine Doctor smiled in approval and told me that I had slain the great beast with the sound of the sacred song of the spirit home. "You have done well," he said, "for the cougar was evil."

I shook my head. "No, it cannot be true. There can be no evil in the spirit home."

I put my lips once again to my flute and played the sacred song of the spirit home. There was another flash of light, and the body of the cougar was transformed into a beautiful spirit maiden all clothed in white skins, the Shining One that some hail as the White Buffalo Woman.

When she spoke to me, her lovely voice sounded very much like the soft notes of a flute: "Child of Dust, you have made yourself holy. You have received the power to change evil into good. You have received the power to restore life to the sick and the dying. Your very breath is now blessed by the spirits."

The beautiful Shining One held up a large stone. "Test the power of your breath!"

I breathed the wakan/mana upon the stone, and the force of my breath made a hole right through it.

The spirit beings cheered me and began to chant that I would now be able to cure pain and illness with the very power of my breath.

The Medicine Doctor said that I could now return to a human life on earth to become a great and powerful sacred teacher and Shaman. It seemed at first as if I were falling through water. For a time I could not breathe properly—and then I entered a warm lodge. From faraway in the spirit home up above, I heard a voice say, "You must stay here for a little while."

Soon I was made to understand that I was dwelling in my new human mother's womb. It was from here that I was born again into earth life. But even at my birth I did not lose my awareness of the time that I had spent in the different animal bodies and the time that I had spent in the spirit home up above. I knew that one day I would be a great Shaman.

The Shaman pauses after he has completed the recitation of his hard-won spiritual credentials. We tell him that we were always certain that he was the sacred teacher whom we sought, but now we are even more impressed with his strength and power and his ability to impart wisdom to us.

At this point we offer the tobacco (or sweet grass) that we have brought.

Before he accepts our gift, he asks us specifically why we have entered his Medicine lodge. What is it that we seek?

Our answer is that we wish to make stronger contact with our spirit helpers. We wish him to provide us with his prayers and his blessings for increased awareness of the powerful beings that manifest their energy as animal totems.

The Shaman nods, accepts our gift, and continues speaking:

You must understand that your gift of tobacco (sweet grass) is really for the spirits up above. When people bring me tobacco or sweet grass, it serves as an energy exchange for the powers that the great spirits offer through me. As I bestow tobacco on the spirits, you must listen carefully so that you may gain power and strength from my words. As you absorb the power of my words, my prayers, and my blessings, you will begin to achieve greater awareness of the true reality that exists all around you.

All I can do, you must truly understand, is to summon the essence of the spirit guardians to begin to open your consciousness. Later, it will be up to you to enter the Silence in order to receive your own teachings from the spirit helpers. It will be up to you to put into practice the spiritual truths that you will be taught.

The Shaman takes a pinch of tobacco between his thumb and forefinger, leans forward, and stretches an arm over the fire that burns between us. As he grinds the tobacco between his fingers, he slowly allows crumbs to fall into the flames. Once again, the Shaman speaks:

Ho! First I offer tobacco to the spirits of the Grandfathers who live in the sacred fire. Listen, O Ancient Ones, to the pleas of these human beings who are now as you once were. This tobacco is yours, O Dwellers of the Dawn Time, and I ask that within three days these supplicants begin to achieve higher and higher awareness.

*Supplicants, receive the spirit energy of the Ancient Ones! May you continue to open to their power, their wisdom, and their teachings!*

Ho! O Buffalo Spirit, I now offer you tobacco, and I ask that you add your strength and wisdom to enlighten and empower these humans. Have mercy on them as you did with me when my spirit lived in your lodge in the body of a buffalo.

After I had fasted and returned from my quest, the White Buffalo Spirit blessed me and gave me spiritual power. I am asking now for you to breathe power upon these humans before you. You promised that you would always do as I desired; therefore, I now ask that these supplicants receive the power of your spirit.

*Supplicants, receive the spirit energy of the Buffalo. May you continue to open to its power, its wisdom, and its teachings!*

Ho! O Bear Spirit, I now offer you tobacco. I ask you to remember the time when I was a spirit and dwelt in your lodge until I was born as a cub. When I lived among your kind, you blessed me and permitted me to study your teachings.

After I had fasted, you granted me the great strength of your wisdom and magic. I am asking now that you breathe power upon these humans who have come here at this time. You promised that you would always do as I desired and that I would be able to transmit your power to whomever I deemed worthy. I ask now that these supplicants before me receive the power of your spirit.

*Supplicants, receive the spirit energy of the Bear. May you continue to open to its power, its wisdom, and its teachings.*

Ho! O Spirit of the Raven, here is your offering of tobacco. When I came to you as a spirit and dwelt in your lodge until I was born as a winged one, you permitted me to study your ways. After I had fasted and returned from my quest, you blessed me and told me that all the spiritual power of your people would be mine to use as I saw fit. I ask now that the supplicants before me receive the power of your spirit.

*Supplicants, receive the spirit energy of the Raven. May you continue to open to its power, its wisdom, and its teachings.*

Ho! O Rattlesnake Spirit, here is your offering of tobacco. I know you remember well when I came to you as a spirit and was later born as one that crawls on his belly. You allowed me to study your ways, and after I had fasted and returned from my quest, you blessed me with your wisdom and a gift of your rattles to shake and drive away all negative spirits.

I am now shaking my rattle before these humans who seek wisdom and enlightenment. You promised me that you would always do my bidding. Grant these supplicants the power of your spirit.

*Supplicants, receive the spirit energy of the Rattlesnake. May you continue to open to its power, its wisdom, and its teachings.*

Ho! O Turtle Spirit, here is your tobacco. You, who bless all those who walk the pathway of peace, I know that you remember well the years I spent among your kind until I was born as one who carries his lodge upon his back. You allowed me to study your ways, and after I had fasted and returned from my quest, you taught me how to achieve peace of heart and spirit and how to remove all pain of body and mind from my being.

You promised never to deny any request that I made of you, so I am asking that you now grant these supplicants before you the proper receptivity to receive the power of your spirit.

*Supplicants, receive the spirit energy of the Turtle. May you continue to open to its power, its wisdom, its teachings.*

Ho! O Shining Ones and Spirits from our original home, you blessed me after I had spent many years as a spirit. You made my flute sacred and granted my music the power to heal, to inspire, to activate the inner spirit of those supplicants who come to me. Here, too, is some tobacco for you.

Keep the night free of all discordant spirit beings for those supplicants who now sit before me. I now direct my breath upon the supplicants to protect them from all the Horrid Things of Darkness that seek to confuse and misdirect the spirit self from its sacred goal.

The Shaman bids us to rise and stand before him. He leans forward and directs his breath and the wakan/mana toward each of us.

And you O Great Mystery, Chief of all the Spirits, you have blessed me with your sacred gift of life. With this gift of tobacco, I thank you for the wisdom and the awarenesses that you have given me throughout my many life experiences as spirit beings—as the raven, the fish, the bear, the turtle, the rattlesnake, the buffalo, and as humans, both male and female.

I ask now that you bless these supplicants and send them each spirit helpers to keep them from wandering away from the path that leads them to the true and original home up above. Keep us all ever secure in the Oneness of your Spirit. Ho-o-o!

We stand, bow our heads in respect, and quietly leave the Medicine lodge. We traveled with the great Shaman through many dimensions of time and space. Through his awareness we entered the life experiences of many different animals. Through his death and rebirth we traveled to the spirit world and the dimension of the Grandparents. He blessed us with the spirit energies of many powerful animal totems.

Let us now undertake a spirit journey of our own.

## The Shaman's Gifts

Use the relaxation process in Chapter 2 to quiet and relax your physical body. Your success in this exercise depends upon your willingness to make contact with the totem animal that serves as your spirit helper and to receive gifts of higher awareness. Be certain that you are in an extremely relaxed state before the voice of a friend—or your own prerecorded voice—leads you through the following exercise:

As your body lies now in a state of deep relaxation, your mind, your Essential Self, is very much aware that you are being surrounded by a beautiful, golden light. You feel the warmth of the light that comes from the Great Mystery and you are becoming more and more at one with the awareness that you are being loved unconditionally by an intelligence who has always loved you just as you are.

You are sensing strongly the presence of an intelligence that you have always known on one level of consciousness. On one level of awareness you have known that this intelligence has been near you ever since you were a child.

You are becoming aware of the sensation of warmth in your chest and on the top of your head. And now you see a ray of light that reaches out to touch your chest. You see that it issues from a bright, golden light that is approaching you.

As you watch, you see that the golden light has acquired a tinge of pink. See the light begin to swirl around you. As you watch, the swirling light now moves slower and slower until you begin to see that it has form and substance.

You are now becoming aware of the shape of a body. At the count of three, you will see clearly that is your spirit helper in the form of your animal totem.

One . . . becoming clearer and clearer. Two . . . clearer and clearer. Three . . . you see clearly before you now your animal totem, your spirit helper. Feel the love that flows out to you from your totem animal's eyes. You feel your body, mind, and spirit becoming even more enveloped in the warmth of unconditional love from your spirit helper.

You have a strong inner knowing that your animal totem has come to guide you to a very special place where you will be able to receive knowledge that will help you to achieve a worthwhile goal. Your animal totem indicates that you should follow it where it will now lead you. Feel its loving vibration. Feel the vibration of one who loves you with pure, spiritual love. Feel the vibration of your spirit helper, who has come to take you to a special place where profound visions await you.

Now you see a purple mist rising up around you as you begin to move through time and space with your totem animal. See the purple mist rise up around you as you move through the sacred portal to the dimension where visions live.

The mist clears, and you and your spirit helper are standing in a holy place.

You may be seeing yourself in a beautiful garden that lies before a majestic temple. You may be seeing yourself in a sacred place in a forest. You may be seeing yourself high on some mountain retreat. You may be seeing yourself standing before a Medicine lodge.

Wherever you are, it is the holy place that you most desire to be. Wherever you are, your totem animal is beside you, guarding you, guiding you.

There is now a vibration in the air as if a flute is playing . . . as if tiny bells are ringing . . . as if beautiful voices are singing. At that signal, a wise Shaman, a sacred teacher, comes to meet you. Your totem animal steps aside to allow the Shaman to embrace you.

See the love in the Shaman's eyes. Look deeply into the eyes of that beloved teacher. As you do so, you will learn the name of this great master teacher. You have the ability to hear the name now! *(Pause here for fifteen seconds)* If you did not hear the name, do not be concerned. It will come to you later in a dream.

Become totally aware of the Shaman. See the teacher's clothes . . . body shape . . . face . . . mouth . . . eyes. Be aware of anything that the Shaman might be holding.

The teacher tells you that he or she has a very special gift of greeting for you, a special gift that will aid you in achieving deep and powerful visions.

He reaches within his robe and brings forth a leather bag. He opens the bag and hands you the gift. You have the ability to see the gift now! *(Pause here for fifteen seconds)* Look at the gift. Take it into your hands. Feel it. Know it. Show the gift to your totem animal. Tell the Shaman how you feel about him and his gift.

And now the Shaman indicates that you should sit with him before a fire that burns brightly before his dwelling place. Be aware that your spirit helper, your totem animal, sits beside you.

The sacred teacher is now telling you that when you look carefully into the flames of the fire, you will be able to see a meaningful vision. The Shaman tells you that you will be able to see a teaching that is meant for your good and your gaining. You will see all that is necessary for your present level of understanding. You will see a vision completely individualized for you and for your particular needs at this time. You have the ability to see the vision now! (*Pause here for approximately two minutes*)

And now your spirit helper, your totem animal, is indicating that it is time to leave the wise Shaman. It is time for your guide to return you to your physical body.

You bid the Shaman farewell, and as you walk with your spirit helper toward the purple mist of time, you turn to your totem animal and ask if you may have a name by which to call your guide. Ask if you might have a name by which you may summon the spiritual vibration of your totem animal at any time. You have the ability to hear your spirit helper's name now! (*Pause here for twenty seconds*)

If you did not hear the name at this time, do not be concerned. It will be revealed to you later during a dream.

And now as you step into the purple mist of time, you feel your Essential Self beginning to return to your physical body. At the count of five, you will return to full consciousness. One . . . becoming awake. Two . . . more and more awake and feeling very good. Three . . . becoming very much awake now. Four . . . becoming more and more awake. Five . . . wide awake and feeling wonderful!

# CHAPTER 4

# Going on Spirit Journeys

A S YOU CONTINUE TO WORK with your animal totem, you will find that your spirit helper will be able to assist you in passing through the mystic portal that leads to a timeless realm existing in a higher spiritual vibration, a dimension where unconditional love, wisdom, and knowledge flow from the Great Mystery. With practice, you will begin to find it easier to join your spirit helper in this beautiful realm where new awarenesses await you.

There will be occasions when your totem animal will convey a teaching to you without words and without an accompanying vision. Yet you will find that those thoughts will create images within your mind as if a living diagram manifested along with them.

When you permit yourself to enter an altered state of consciousness, you must truly wish to receive an awareness or a vision teaching from your spirit helper. You must desire to be taught so that a greater understanding of many of life's problems may then be yours. Such a desire must be uppermost in your heart and mind.

Sometimes we can be pulled on a spirit journey without any warning. We may be actively engaged in mundane, ordinary activity, when, suddenly, we are drawn to that in-between universe, that place-which-exists-everywhere-and-nowhere in a time-outside-of-time, that dimension to which shamans venture to seek holy wisdom and spiritual knowledge. On those occasions, it may be up to us to seek out the full meaning of the teaching that we were to receive from our spirit helper.

And then there are those special occasions when a powerful new spirit helper may reach through the portal and present us with a unique learning experience.

### An Extraordinary Spiritual Adventure

On the evening of December 2, 1974, my soul body was instantly taken to such a place; and even now, twenty-two years later, both the experience and the lessons that I learned from it remain vivid in my mind.

I had been standing speaking with my older son, Bryan, in his bedroom sometime after midnight. I had been feeling healthy and robust all day, and I had absolutely no warning or any kind of advance notice that I was about to undergo an extraordinary spiritual adventure.

Then, in mid-sentence, I suddenly began to feel very strange. I told my son I thought that I had better lie down for a moment in my own room.

There was a whirling blur of motion and a strange kind of humming sound, and I was standing in a place very different from our old Iowa farmhouse. It appeared to be some kind of arena or outdoor auditorium. There was a bright sun overhead, and I could hear what sounded like thousands of voices shouting and screaming.

I did not even have time to clear my senses from my sudden arrival in the arena when someone or something struck a fierce blow to my head from my left side. My face crunched into coarse sand as I fell heavily to the floor of the arena.

The moment that I sprawled face down, I heard what sounded like multitudes of men and women cheering and laughing at my having been knocked so roughly and completely off my feet. And I could clearly distinguish choruses of voices shouting for my death: "Kill him! We've got him now! Kill him!"

It was terrible to hear thousands of voices shouting for my death. My poor confused brain was trying desperately to make sense of what was happening to me.

Was I having a past life recall of a prior existence as a gladiator? No, I reasoned, because I was not seeing a memory being reenacted in a trancelike state. I was feeling it happening in the present.

Had I suddenly been transported to some alternate reality? I sincerely hoped not, because it appeared that I was about to be terminated.

I tried to get to my feet, but a heavy foot slammed itself into my back, forcing my face back into the coarse sand of the arena. Once again, the crowd cheered wildly at my humiliation.

Over my left shoulder I looked toward the stands which I supposed held the evil masses of scum who were screaming for my death. But although I could all too clearly and distinctly hear the raucous cries for my death, I could see absolutely no one sitting in the stands. There was only a kind of dark, swirling mist hanging over the empty rows of seats.

Once again, I tried to regain my feet and was pushed roughly back down by what felt like the heel of a very large boot.

"Enough of this," an authoritative voice shouted from somewhere in the arena, "He has been defeated. Kill him if he cannot get to his feet!"

I certainly felt defeated. I was lying pitched forward on my face in an arena in some unknown aspect of reality. I felt as though I truly were a bested gladiator. I felt whipped, mangled, destroyed—and that obviously pleased a lot of unseen and bloodthirsty entities who were hungry for my soul.

The Viking spirit in me really hated to check out without having put up a damn good fight, but I had been knocked down from behind by some powerful foe before I had a chance to defend myself.

While I lay there, dissatisfied with my fate, but helplessly awaiting my powerful unseen opponent's final blow, I became aware of another chorus of voices that had suddenly manifested and had begun to shout down those malevolent beings who were so ecstatic over my miserable, battered condition.

"Get up!" they were shouting at me. "Get up! You can do it! Put your legs under you. Breathe deeply. Make your chest move in and out. Breathe! Live! You can do it!"

At their words of encouragement, I felt energized. I was no longer resigned to lie there helplessly and await my fate. I would stand up and face my foe.

For every movement I made, there were excited shouts of encouragement to keep going and angry curses demanding that I give in to my ignominious death in the arena.

I was so weak. I needed help.

Then a figure moved from the shadows. I had not previously noticed her because she was as dark as the shaded area in which she had stood, but it was apparent that she had been there quietly watching my ordeal from its very beginning. The entity's ebony body was unmistakably that of a tall, muscular woman, but her head, her features, were those of a lioness.

She stood before me, a creature of remarkable beauty and fierce destruction. Was it she who had come to destroy me?

She did not open her mouth, but I heard her strong voice inside my head: *You made the decision to fight, to resist evil. I will protect you.*

She reached out a hand and pulled me to my feet, and as she did so, those entities who had encouraged me—whoever or whatever they were—gave out a mighty cheer of triumph.

The lionheaded woman opened her mouth to speak, and her words were like powerful bolts of electricity that shook my entire body: *Remember this time. Find the learning in it.*

In the next few moments, I became dimly aware of someone else holding my hand, calling my name. It was another woman. A human woman with a human face. But she seemed unable to touch me. We seemed separated by an invisible barrier. Several more powerful shocks set my physical body to vibrating like a tuning fork.

And then the woman holding my hand became my wife, Marilyn. The statuesque, lionheaded woman was gone, and so was the ancient arena and the screaming, cheering invisible multitudes. I was lying on my bed, although I still seemed to have the sand of the arena in my mouth. For another few minutes, periodic shocks of energy from that in-between universe continued to stiffen my body.

Marilyn insisted that Bryan call an ambulance. I tried to explain that I was all right, that I had just been taken somewhere on a spirit journey for a teaching. I really felt embarrassed that the ambulance crew would be called to our farmhouse over ten miles from the hospital on a cold December night, but I could also understand how a wife and son would feel if their husband and father had just suddenly collapsed in a heap at their feet.

I passed all the physical tests with high marks, as I was certain that I would, and I knew that the true challenge lay in passing my spiritual tests with good grades.

Marilyn, who passed from this world on another cold December night in 1982, was able to see that my spirit journey had changed my outlook on life in many ways, both major and minute. Close friends were able to perceive that I had undergone a significant kind of rebirth experience. In fact, a number of them had even picked up on my encounter with the lionheaded entity in their own dreams and visions.

During that period of my spiritual quest, I had begun a rather strict daily regimen structured around the Medicine teachings that had been so generously bestowed upon me by traditional practitioners from many different tribes. My eclectic cosmology had easily blended with the symbology of Native American Medicine Power. I knew that my totem animals were the wolf, the dog, the owl, and the crow. Sun Bear had added another for me when he explained that my birth sign on the Medicine Wheel was that of the cougar, the mountain lion.

I toyed with the idea that my lionheaded lady had stepped out of the Medicine Wheel to come to my aid, but that didn't feel quite right. My sense of her kept bringing me back to ancient Egypt.

I have always been fascinated by prehistory. Armchair archaeology has been a passion of mine since childhood. I cannot remember a time when I have not loved exploring the mysteries of the past, theorizing about lost civilizations, and arguing about Homo sapiens' true role in the universal scheme of things; but prior to this time I had never really been greatly intrigued by the colorful ancient Egyptian hierarchy of gods.

And then one night as I paged through one of my reference books, I saw my lionheaded protector. Her name was Sekhmet. I read on in total fascination:

Sekhmet, one of the most ancient of deities, came into Egypt in a time unrecorded from a place that is unknown. Sekhmet, known as "Lady of the Place of the Beginning of Time" and "One Who Was Before the Gods Were," was esteemed as a goddess of enormous power, a defender of the gods against all forces of evil.

Sovereign of Her Father, Ra. Lady of Flame. Lady of the Lamp. Great One of Magic. The solar disc on her hand signifies her control of the sun. As consort of her husband-brother Ptah, the creative process, Sekhmet is the one found most beautiful by Art itself.

It is said that no other Egyptian deity was represented by so many statues. The priests of Sekhmet were for centuries regarded as the most potent healers and magicians of the ancient world, due, perhaps, to their utilization of trance states.

But Sekhmet had a dual nature. By her control of the sun, she made the crops grow, but she also manifested droughts. She was a goddess of love and war, healing and pestilence, cursing and blessing.

There was no question that in dealing with Sekhmet one had to maintain balance at all times. And you had better accentuate the positive, for she was always known as the most potentially dangerous of the Egyptian deities. Magicians and priests who sought power knew well that the greatest source of all lay in Sekhmet. They also knew that they had nothing to fear as long as they emphasized their own positive aspects and did nothing to provoke her ferocious wrath.

I was somewhat overwhelmed as I read the awesome dossier on the entity who had offered me a helping hand when I had lain battered in the sands of an arena that existed in some unknown dimension of time and space. Part of her admonition to me to learn from the experience was beginning to become clearer to me. Somewhere in an in-between universe, a time-outside-of-time, such archetypal beings as Sekhmet maintained an existence independent of our linear time and our physical universe. It was a place where visions and representations of totemic powers lived with an intensity that would vibrate throughout the infinity of space and the eternity of time.

While I was puzzling all these things through, I ran across one of Robert E. L. Masters' research papers, "Consciousness and Extra-Ordinary Phenomena," in which he describes an experiment he conducted wherein a female subject had activated an archetype or symbol system. The system that the experiment activated was the Egyptian Goddess Sekhmet and her world.

For many years, Bob Masters and his wife, Jean Houston, had generously supplied me with copies of their research papers and information about various projects originating from their Foundation for Mind Research in Pomona, New York. And now I read with fascination Masters' report that the research subject had returned again and again "to another reality or Imaginal World, bringing back exhaustive accounts of her experiences."

The experiment, he stressed, had nothing to do with a regression to a supposed past-life experience, with traveling back in time, or anything of that sort. Rather, he said it had to do with "the intentional activation of, or awakening to, something which has its own reality in present time; or perhaps it could be better said that it is from our own present time that we enter into its own nontemporal reality."

In November of 1975, I made an appointment with Bob Masters to discuss Sekhmet's domain and the world of archetypes, and I traveled from my home in Iowa to The Foundation for Mind Research in Pomona, New York. Synchronicity blessed me when I arrived as Jean Houston presented me with the delightful news that Michele Carrier, the art student who had been the subject in the Sekhmet experiments, had unexpectedly arrived for a visit.

After a warm exchange of greetings, we settled down in comfortable chairs for a discussion of a separate reality that coexisted with our own. I asked Michele where she believed Sekhmet's world to exist.

After a moment of reflection, she answered that it probably existed somewhere between our physical, three-dimensional world and the archetypal world. "Sekhmet always called it a 'two-dimensional world,'" she said, "because it is not an imaginary world and yet it's not concrete in terms of everyday reality. I think her world lies someplace between archetype and history, someplace between the collective and the individual unconscious."

Masters explained why he chose to center the experiment on Sekhmet. "It was because of the number of very unusual experiences that people had with statues of the Goddess Sekhmet that I had in my possession—and also the fact that the figure is a very sympathetic one to me."

He went on to tell how he would sometimes leave people in a room with a statue of Sekhmet and return to find that they had gone into trance with it spontaneously, without any kind of suggestion, and had very rich experiences.

There had also been occasions in which he had been conducting a hypnosis session in a room where the statue was, and Sekhmet would steal his hypnotic subject away from him. Suddenly they were no longer in trance with him; they were in trance with Sekhmet; and when they returned to wakefulness, they would tell him all about it.

"In Egypt, where they always worked with statues and images of the gods, there is a phenomenon called Hanu, which means 'being seized by the god,'" Masters explained. "It means that the god reaches out and grabs you. And Sekhmet was reaching out and grabbing people in the best, ancient Egyptian tradition—and so I wanted to explore it."

Briefly, I summarized the story of how Sekhmet had reached out and grabbed me that December night almost a year before.

Although Bob Masters had worked with dozens of people who had experienced Sekhmet's world more or less completely, he found in Michele Carrier a natural mystic whose ability for interacting with Sekhmet's dimension went beyond all the others. Her experiences proved to be so profound that the experiments continued for a year and a half.

Michele very much intrigued me when she commented that sometimes she, too, had been a lioness in Sekhmet's kingdom.

"I had to fight some lionesses once," she said. "I was put in the center of a group of old lionesses, and I had to fight with one of them. If I lost, it was the end. And then after I did win, I was sent off to do another task."

Masters said that Michele had to undergo many ordeals, which generally were functioning at several levels.

"For example, there's a mythological dimension and then also a psychological one," he explained. "If she achieved success in an ordeal, such as fighting a demon and overcoming him, then this was reflected not only in her further advance along the path of initiation in the world of Sekhmet, but it also meant that psychological changes would take place in her everyday life."

Obviously trial by ordeal was de rigueur in Sekhmet's kingdom, for I, too, had been seized by the goddess and unceremoniously dumped in an arena to be pummeled by a powerful unseen adversary. My success in the ordeal, with her intervention, had definitely set in motion a number of psychological changes in my everyday life. And, of course, the vivid experience had given me another dramatic proof that worlds and realities beyond our own dimension do exist.

Michele said that she had once been told that Sekhmet could only work in the relationship between them. "I think that Sekhmet is a historical representation of the archetype of the feminine. . . . Sekhmet is like a mediator for energy; she is a form for it to come through.

"Sekhmet exists within the collective unconscious," she continued. "There is no status to the collective unconscious apart from us. Sekhmet comes from a primitive state in the evolution of consciousness, but the symbols that are there can evolve within the consciousness of someone today. They may be primitive symbols, but they are still active symbols. The same archetypes that cavemen were dealing with, we're dealing with now; but we're dealing with them in a different way."

Masters pointed out that if one were to study the psychology of idols and the representation of gods in the ancient world, it becomes apparent that many of them were designed to alter human consciousness and to become a means whereby communication could be established with the deity.

"These idols were—and Michele once used the words—keys of space," he said. "They're ways into the world of the gods. I've worked with figures of other deities in my exploration of this ancient psychology, and many of them will work. People can go into trance with them. They can go into their worlds and begin to live in them."

What, I asked, did he believe to be the mechanism involved in the kind of phenomenon that we had experienced with Sekhmet.

"Sekhmet is able to effect a process of individuation in people who work with her," he said. "They experience real psychological growth and maturation. And such experience has the quality of the numinous. So in that sense, Sekhmet would seem to bestow authentic religious experience and archetypal experience.

"Once many years ago, Sekhmet showed me images that she described as cosmic 'toys' that had been scattered around the universe, functioning as teaching instruments. Her image was one of them. Wherever her image was found it would initiate in the human psyche a whole unfolding of knowledge."

So it is with the image of one's animal totem. It, too, serves as a teaching instrument that initiates a whole unfolding of knowledge in the human psyche. The archetypal image of the animal totem also has its more complete expression in the higher reality that exists between the collective and the individual unconscious.

The animal totems are ancient symbols that remain active and valid within evolving human consciousness. They are activators of the unconscious. They are doorways to the dimension of spirit—and when you take your spirit journeys through the exercises in this book, you will discover another world that is more vivid, more beautiful, more real, than any other that you have ever known.

## A SHAMAN'S SPIRIT JOURNEY THROUGH THE EYES OF ANIMALS

Internationally known metaphysician, author, and teacher Tara Sutphen has served as an accomplished guide during dozens of journeys into the mystical world of totems and Shamans at seminars that she conducts with her husband, Dick. The Sutphens also have a publishing company, and their son Scott owns The Malibu Shaman bookstore in Malibu, California. Tara generously provided me with the following spirit journey in which the supplicant may face fears and find his or her goals while experiencing increased awareness through the senses of various totem animals.*

* © Tara Sutphen and Valley of the Sun Publishing Company.

Once again, use the relaxation process provided in Chapter 2 or use any other technique that you wish to place yourself in a very relaxed physical state—and in a very receptive frame of mind. You may read the following spirit journey aloud, pausing now and then to allow its energy to permeate your consciousness. Or, as previously suggested, you may have a friend or family member read the relaxation process and the visualization to you. Or, as I have pointed out, you may prefer recording your own voice reading these exercises, using the tape as your guide to expanding awareness.

After you have placed yourself in a state of deep and peaceful relaxation through one of the processes suggested above, join Tara Sutphen on her Shaman Journey:

> Breathe deeply and relax completely. Breathe through your nose and exhale through your mouth. Very deeply . . . very, very deeply. Feel calm and peaceful. Relaxed and at ease. Calm and peaceful. Relaxed and at ease. (*Repeat two or three times*)
>
> Now imagine yourself outside in the country on a clear summer night. The sky is full of stars, and it feels good to be here. You feel safe and secure as you look up at the blanket of stars. You hear the sounds of the night. Imagine this very, very vividly. Be there. (*Pause one minute*)
>
> It feels so good to be here looking up at the stars and enjoying the night. And now it's time to draw down the universal energy of the stars, so please imagine yourself drawing down the light, drawing down the energy of the stars, the positive powers of the universe. Perceive this energy as being drawn down in the form of an illumination that enters your crown chakra on the top of your head. Do this now. Draw down the energy and allow it to become your reality.
>
> (Softly) The universal energy of the stars . . . draw down the light . . . the positive powers of the universe . . . the God Light . . . the Star Light . . . the Love Light . . . let it happen. Let it be. Draw down the universal energy of the stars . . . the Light of the Universe. (*Pause one minute*)
>
> You are now filled with light, and you look to the eastern horizon to see the sky becoming lighter and lighter and lighter.

And as the sun rises, you offer thanks for all that you have and all that you may become. (*Pause one minute*)

The sun is now above the horizon, and it feels warm on your skin. You notice a trail off to your right. Follow this trail, for it will lead you to a beautiful meadow and a Native American Shaman who awaits you. Go ahead. Follow the trail until you come to the meadow and meet the Medicine Man who will serve as your guide on this journey. (*Pause one minute*)

And now as you perceive the meadow and the Shaman, feel him take your hand in friendship. See the kindness in his eyes. Open to his loving energy. He's been waiting here for you. He'll be guiding you on your journey, and he'll give you some important items to take along with you.

Walk with him now. Walk with the Shaman to his teepee, which stands nearby. Go along with him now. Make yourself comfortable in his teepee. Visualize the teepee very, very vividly. (*Pause thirty seconds*)

You are now sitting in the teepee across from the Shaman. He shares a cup of water with you, saying, "Water symbolizes the sustenance of all life." Go ahead and drink the water. (*Pause ten seconds*)

You are relaxed and at ease, and it feels good to be sitting in the teepee. And now the Shaman lights a peace pipe and exhales the smoke as a symbol of brotherhood. You observe, and then he passes the pipe to you. You lift the pipe to your lips, then exhale the symbol of brotherhood, opening your heart chakra in the process. Feel it happening. (*Pause ten seconds*)

The Shaman hands you a pouch and tells you that this is for collecting objects and messages on your journey. Accept the pouch.

Now the Shaman marks the center of your forehead with the sacred ashes. As his finger touches your third eye, he says, "This gives you the power of the seer. On your journey you will see through the eyes of animals—and you will be able to feel what the animal is experiencing."

Now it is time to leave the teepee and set out on your journey. Step outside where two horses wait. The Shaman accompanies you. Imagine yourself mounting one of the horses. Take a moment to pat your horse and get to know him. This horse will carry you on a journey to personal freedom.

The Shaman raises his Medicine stick into the air and says, "South. We will ride south to seek your pleasures."

Now you are riding across the terrain. Imagine the landscape very vividly. What is it like? (*Pause five seconds*)

What is the weather? (*Pause five seconds*) How fast are you traveling? (*Pause five seconds*)

You are now riding into a wooded area. Perceive the woods very vividly. Ahead of you on the trail, a deer steps out of the trees and stops directly in front of you. You also stop and look at the deer. You look at the Shaman. He smiles and nods at you. You have the power of the seer. You have the power to become the deer. Feel yourself merging your consciousness with the deer's consciousness. (*Pause five seconds*)

You are the deer standing on the trail looking at two riders on horseback. It's time to go and you bolt off. You are the deer. You run down the trail, running more gracefully than you ever dreamed possible. You are the deer! You are the deer, and you feel a sense of excitement that you've never felt before. Go ahead! Run all on your own . . . run . . . run . . . run! (*Pause ten seconds*)

As you are running, the natural environment fades away, and you are running past the people, places, and things that you most enjoy in life . . . those things that give you satisfaction and generate self-esteem. See those people, places, and things very vividly. (*Pause one minute*)

Ahead is a beautiful field of flowers. Run into the field. Here among the flowers you will find a special message about the people, places, and things that bring you pleasure. Stop and nose around in the flowers and find the object and the message. Find them. What is the object? What is the message? (*Pause twenty seconds*)

You hear the Medicine Man calling your name—and you are instantly back on your horse, riding beside the Shaman. Mentally you place the object and the message that you found among the flowers in your pouch.

"East," the Shaman says. "We ride East to seek knowledge." And again you are riding. You feel at one with your horse as you travel over the countryside. Observe the terrain . . . the weather . . . the speed of your horse. (*Pause ten seconds*)

Ahead you see an eagle sitting in a treetop. Ride toward the eagle. (*Pause five seconds*) The Shaman reins in his horse and points his Medicine stick at the eagle. "The eagle will lead you to knowledge," the Shaman says. "Become the eagle!"

You look to the eagle as he lifts off the tree limb, and in that moment you feel the wind in your feathers, the strain in your muscles, and you realize that you have become the eagle. Go ahead and fly free. Be the eagle. Be the eagle. Fly . . . fly . . . fly! (*Pause ten seconds*)

As the eagle, you know what you seek to accomplish in your life. And now you are going to sweep down and perceive what you need to accomplish your goals. Trust your insights and visualization as you begin sweeping down to observe what you need to do to accomplish your goals. (*Pause one minute*)

Feel the wind in your feathers. Feel yourself rising up on the air currents. Higher . . . higher . . . Now swoop down again, down, down toward that glinting object way down below. There is a message for you there. A message about your goals and how to accomplish them. Fly down and perceive the object and its message. (*Pause twenty seconds*) You now have the message and the object and you mentally place them in your pouch.

The Shaman calls you again to return to him. You find yourself once again on horseback, riding like the wind. The Shaman says, "North. It's time to ride north to examine your burdens." And again you feel at one with the horse as you travel over the countryside. Observe the terrain . . . the weather . . . the speed of your horse. (*Pause ten seconds*)

You ride until you come to a wooded and rocky terrain. You rein in the horses near a large outcropping of rocks. The Shaman directs you to sit on the rocks. Go ahead. Dismount. Walk over and sit on the rocks. (*Pause five seconds*)

The Shaman begins to apply war paint to your face. Allow him to prepare you for a battle with your fears. (*Pause five sec-*

*onds*) As he finishes, a bear emerges about twenty yards away. The bear sees you, stands on his back legs, and roars.

And in that moment, you become the bear. You perceive yourself roaring at two humans sitting on the rocks. You feel yourself turning away, skirting the rocks and breaking through the brush. You feel your great muscles and your lumbering body as you move quickly away. Go ahead—experience the bear. Experience the bear! (*Pause ten seconds*)

As you move through the terrain, you begin to perceive all of the burdens that you feel weigh you down and keep you from being all that you are capable of being. Perceive these burdens very, very vividly now. (*Pause one minute*)

Now, up ahead in a thicket, you see an object and a message that can help you. Perceive the message and the object and mentally put them in your pouch.

The Shaman calls your name, and once again you find yourself on horseback, riding into a beautiful, peaceful meadow. The Shaman dismounts and spreads a blanket on the ground. Join him. Help him spread the blanket.

As the horses graze, you sit down on the blanket facing the Shaman. He says, "It is time to look at the objects and the messages that you've received on this journey."

He smiles and points at your pouch. "What object and message did you obtain as the eagle in the east, where you sought knowledge of your goals?"

Show him and explain. (*Pause one minute*)

And now he asks, "What object and message did you obtain as the bear in the north, where you sought awareness of your burdens?"

Show him and explain. (*Pause one minute*)

And now you ask the Shaman, "What about the west?" The Shaman replies, "The west is your trail of expanded awareness. Follow it on your own with an open heart."

You stand up and draw a gift out of your pouch and give it to the Shaman. See clearly what it is. (*Pause five seconds*)

Bidding the Shaman good-bye, you mount your horse and begin to travel west. Allow it to happen. Feel it happening. You ride like the wind . . . westward . . . into expanded awareness . . . success . . . and good health. You're riding west to become all that you are capable of being. You're riding west, remembering everything that you experienced in this peaceful meditation.

On the count of five, you will awaken filled with joy, at peace with yourself, the world, and everyone in it. Number One, coming on up and remembering everything. Number Two, coming on up a little more. Number Three, coming on up now, feeling balance and harmony. Number Four, recall the situation and the place that you are in. Number Five, wide awake . . . wide awake!

When you have returned to full consciousness after receiving vision teachings from such spiritual exercises as the one just presented, you must decide if the lessons that you have acquired are meant only for your own personal growth or if you have received universal teachings that are meant to be shared with others. If your spirit helper has presented you with an insight or a truth that would benefit other initiates on the spiritual path, then you must not permit the power of your vision to stagnate. You *must* share it with others.

In the sharing of your vision teaching, you will come more fully to understand that which you have received from your spirit helper. Each time you relay your vision to another, you will be able to describe it more vividly. Each time you share your teaching, you will remember its lessons in even greater detail. The more you give of your spiritual blessings, the more profound messages you will receive from your spirit helper.

# CHAPTER 5

# Catching and Retrieving Dream Teachings

THE DREAM STATE CAN BE an excellent place for a meaningful dialogue with your spirit helper, and you can begin to program yourself to have such an experience as soon as you get up in the morning.

Begin with your first conscious and prayerful activity by making a positive affirmation that you will meet with your animal totem, your spirit helper, in a meaningful dream that night when you retire. Affirm that you will speak with your spirit helper and that you will receive an important teaching.

From time to time throughout the day, quiet yourself, if even for a moment, and give recognition to the Great Mystery that exists above you, all around you, and within you. Visualize a golden light that connects you to the Great Mystery. The more profoundly you can visualize this connection, the greater will be the results of your dream interaction with your totem guide.

At another time throughout the day, find a moment to quiet yourself and focus your thoughts on the image of your spirit helper. Feel the loving energy of your guide move above you, all around you, and within you. Visualize yourself connected to your spirit helper by a blue ray of light. The more profoundly you can visualize this connection, the greater will be the results of your dream interaction with your totem guide.

It is truly important that you visualize and attempt to feel the reality of the individualized presence of your spirit helper. Know that it is connected to you by a stream of love-energy that flows everlastingly between you.

Several times a day before seeking a profound dream interaction between you and your spirit helper, direct your attention to the Great Mystery and send your love to that holy presence. Remember that the summoning of a teaching dream or a vision must always be as the result of a desire balanced with spirit.

When you retire at night to have your dream encounter, visualize the image of your animal totem preparing to join you in a personal power place. Visualize a lovely clearing in a forest, a picturesque mountain trail, a lonely stretch of beach—wherever you would most like to spend a time in meaningful dialogue with your spirit helper. Know that you have the ability to have a profound dream experience.

If you wish, you may prerecord the relaxation technique provided in Chapter 2 as an added inducement to set you on the path to a significant dream encounter.

There may be occasions when you will awaken in the night and know that you have been receiving dream teachings. You may feel distressed when you become aware that you have been unable to retain the full importance and meaning of the dream.

In these instances, call out to your totem animal, your spirit helper, to help you recover the full understanding of that which the

Great Mystery wishes you to know. Ask that you receive again the full power of the dream teaching that has just been entrusted to you. Visualize your totem animal running after the vision and returning to you with its teaching message fully intact.

Do not permit yourself to become angry or frustrated with yourself for having permitted the teaching message to have become lost to your waking consciousness.

If you should be unable to recall the lesson on that particular evening, begin to prepare yourself upon arising the very next morning with the transmissions of love to the Great Mystery and your spirit helper that I have just described. Then, before falling asleep that night, call upon the Great Mystery to send its mighty energy into your body, mind, and spirit. Charge yourself to return with the vital substance of the dream teachings that you shall receive anew. Ask your spirit helper to stand watch over you so that only good enters into your reception of the teachings.

Remember that any time your totem animal appears in a dream it is a signal for you to take careful notice of a series of important symbols that will be certain to follow. These symbols have been designed by your spirit helper to provide you with vital clues that will aid you in making the right decisions in any matter that may be troubling you. Analyze these symbols with the utmost care.

## TAKING YOUR ANIMAL DREAM SYMBOLS SERIOUSLY

Tara Sutphen told me that whenever animal symbology enters her dreams, she pays very close attention.

"In December of 1994, I dreamed that I had a beloved dog, a blue merle collie, that had his leg ripped off by a bear. Coyotes were following him as he dragged himself home to my Dad and me. We made him comfortable, petted him, and wished him well as he died."

At the time, Tara's father was very ill and had been in and out of the hospital. This is how she interpreted the dream of the wounded and dying collie.

"My Dad and I both loved dogs, and since dogs represent loyalty and friendship, the collie lay dying between us. The bear is a sign of burdens, and the fact that it hurt and maimed the collie indicated a disease or an accident. The burden was Dad's disease, and it was going to take something away from both of us. Coyotes are full of surprises and tricks, perhaps signifying my father coming out of his coma. At the end of my dream, the collie was surrounded by love as he went into the next phase of existence."

A few weeks later, Tara had another dream in which her father was driving a small car down a hill when a black panther ran into the middle of the road.

"In the dream, Dad thought that he had struck the panther with his car, so in his weakened state, he got out and found the big cat lying on the road. When he reached down to see if the panther was still alive, the animal reached up to play with Dad's hand.

"At this time, my father was coming in and out of consciousness, and my brothers and I had moved him into a nursing facility with skilled personnel. Decoding my dream, I saw that the black panther was leading Dad into death, but was toying with him as he went 'downhill,' referring to his steadily worsening condition."

Tara's father had always joked during his illness that he was going to take the last bus to the other world. It appeared that that bus was coming ever closer.

"The night before he died, as I was falling asleep, I vividly felt myself falling toward a green spot. I came closer and closer until I reached out to touch it. All of a sudden it croaked, and I realized that it was a frog. I jumped awake, startling my dog sleeping next to the bed, causing her to jump to her feet.

"Frogs are the symbol for the cleansing of our souls. If I would have touched it, the frog would have indicated a personal sickness for me. But since it croaked, it was warning me about another's illness.

"My father died the next afternoon, seven hours before turning sixty-nine years old. The number 69 is the symbol of yin/yang, perfect balance. The frog is the fetus rebirthing into the next world. Perfect omens for his metaphysician daughter."

## THE LIZARD AS KEEPER OF THE DREAMSTATE

L. Dean Woodruff, an animal totem reader from Las Vegas, was one of thirteen orphaned children of a full blooded Native American woman who were given up for adoption or placed with foster families.

"Though my mother's family was never made known to us," Dean told me, "her heritage has been a strong influence in my life. Because of that strong Mother Earth energy, I have grown to accept the beauty in all living creatures."

Throughout all of his travels, including time spent in the military, Dean continued to encounter lizards. "Wherever I went, I seemed to be found by them and they appeared to be letting me know that I was in safe territory. Now, after twenty-three years in Las Vegas, the lizards and I live with each other. According to the traditions of my mother's people, the lizard is the keeper of the dreamstate, and most of the information that I receive has been in dreams at night."

Using his own totem animals as examples, Dean told me how he would explain their importance in the cosmology of his tradition:

The animal of the East informs you of the challenges that you most need to overcome. My animal of the east is the Ant, which represents patience. Since I have turned so much over to Spirit, my patience has improved a great deal.

The animal of the South protects the child in each of us and keeps innocence balanced within. My animal of the South is the Frog, which represents cleansing. When I wish to become the child again, all I need to do is to find something new and different, and I can see life clean and fresh again.

The animal of the West represents the inner and personal truth for which we all seek to accomplish our goals. My animal of the West is the Lizard, and my dreams have been a very important part of my life. The spirits sometimes make me fall asleep at odd times so they may speak to me.

The animal of the North gives us our greatest wisdom. My animal of the North is the Coyote; and although he is the great trickster, he is also one of the few animals that combines the traits of many others. He can laugh at himself and at others and he reminds us not to take ourselves too seriously. His greatest enemy is usually himself.

The animal from Above is one that guards our dreamtime to keep us in touch with the Star Beings that we are. My creature from Above is the Hummingbird. This totem brings me joy, and it is through joy that I grow both in spirit and in mind.

The animal from Below is the creature that keeps us grounded to this dimension on Mother Earth. My totem from Below is the Owl. The Owl helps me to look past deceptions in life and see the true reality and not what others may wish me to see. Since I am a person who deals too much from the heart, Owl has helped me through many situations.

The animal from Within is the one that governs the heart, and mine is the Possum. The Possum is skilled at diversions that may protect the heart from those who are not operating from integrity or pure love. The great Possum has come into my life many times to divert myself from those who are not true.

Dean said that the animal of the Right Side is the totem that represents our masculine side, while the animal of the Left Side is the totem of the feminine side. The male pushes us forward in life; the female nurtures us along the way.

"Each morning before I meditate," he said, "I go outside and face the East and thank Grandfather and Grandmother for the dreams I have received. Then I thank and bless all the creatures that so bless me daily. I would be at a great loss if animals were not in my life. I simply cannot imagine them not guiding me daily."

## HOLDING ON TO YOUR DREAMS

Some Medicine practitioners like to have at their bedside a physical symbol of their ability to catch and hold on to their dreams. These Medicine Dream Hoops, popularly called "Dream Catchers," represent the web of life. Bad dreams are caught in the web and dissipate in the first light of dawn. Good dreams pass through the center hole and are caught by the dreamer's psyche, thus to be fulfilled in his or her destiny. Any symbol that appeals to the individual dreamer, such as a totem animal, may be painted upon the shield that surrounds the center opening.

While the Dream Catcher is primarily a physical stimulus to encourage the unconscious to remember dreams, another more tangible method of holding onto your dream teachings from your spirit helper is that of keeping a dream diary.

- Immediately upon awakening, jot down your dream on a note pad or dictate it into a tape recorder.

- Never wait until later to jot down the dream, for by the time that you put on your slippers and sit down to breakfast, important dream details may be gone. Write the dream down before you get out of bed. Of course, if you should wake up during the night, capture any dream that is fresh in your mind then, too. Don't wait until morning.

- Keep the notations simple. Write down the date, what the dream was about, and then leave a space for interpretation. Don't be concerned with your penmanship or spelling. Just get the highlights of the dream on paper or tape. Later, if it is a significant dream, you can flesh it out.

- Unless an instant and logical meaning to the dream should come immediately to mind, put your notations away until you have more time to give it serious consideration. If the symbolism confuses you, go into the Silence and seek deeper answers within.

When author-researcher Dr. Stanley Krippner was the director of the Dream Laboratory at Maimonides Hospital in Brooklyn, New York, some years back, he described one primitive Malay tribe that encouraged each family member to discuss his or her dreams at breakfast so that other members of the family might offer their interpretations.

"This type of constant examination of the inner life makes it easy for dreams to be remembered," Dr. Krippner said. "It may also help to account for the fact that this tribe does not engage in warfare. In addition, theft and mental illness are virtually unknown among tribal members.

"By paying closer attention to one's dreams, an individual may gain a greater access to his inner life and, thereby, become a more sensitive, a more fully functioning individual."

When I asked Dr. Krippner for his suggestions for helping people to remember dreams that might be speaking uniquely of the inner life, he responded with the following:

1. When you first awaken in the morning, lie quietly before jumping out of bed. Let your mind dwell on the first thing that pops into it. Do not allow daytime interests to interrupt.

Your first waking thought may remind you of the contents of your last dream before awakening. You may need to try this technique several mornings in a row in order to get results.

2. Keep a notebook of the dreams you do remember for a month. Look for important ideas or themes running through the dreams. You may discover that you have been working on a problem at night without being aware of it. You may even find instances in which your dreams suggested actions that you actually were able to carry out later.

3. Look for items in your dreams that might be symbolic of something. Get the opinion of your family and friends.

4. Look for puns in your dreams—a play on words, a play on numbers.

5. Before you go to sleep at night, review the work you have done on a problem or on a question that has you stumped. If you have given the problem enough presleep attention, you may find upon awakening in the morning that you remember a dream in which the possible solution appeared. This is one way of encouraging creative dreams.

6. Keep dream diaries. Record your dreams for six months or a year. Try to get other members of your family or circle of friends to do the same. Determine as best you can which dreams reflect personal problems, which dreams involve national or international events, and which dreams are highly symbolic.

## A Mini-Dictionary of Animal Totem Dream Symbols

I have included a mini-dictionary of animal totem dream symbols in this chapter with the admonition that you use it only as an aid in assisting you to arrive at your own personal interpretations of dream symbology. Truly, you are the only one who can determine precisely what your animal totem represents in your dream scenario, because the dream is meant for you.

Before you refer to this dictionary of possible dream interpretations, please try your very best to analyze for yourself exactly what the animal symbol in your dream was attempting to tell you. If you feel totally perplexed over the meaning of the appearance of your animal totem in a dream, then use this dictionary as a reference, a catalyst that may spark a personal revelation of that particularly troublesome imagery.

Because this dictionary is intended to be used only as a kind of mental trigger to fire your own thoughts into full realization, the individual definitions are very brief. For additional clues, refer to the detailed Totem Animal Dictionary beginning on page 151.

**Alligator**—If your dream showed you in a boat with many alligators approaching, your totem animal may be warning you that enemies of a physical or spiritual nature may soon appear on your earthwalk.

**Ant**—Your spirit helper may be reminding you of the virtues of industriousness.

**Antelope**—Your dream of an antelope may be advising you to take another approach to the problem before you.

**Ape**—You may soon be facing an opponent in the workplace or a rival for the affections of a loved one.

**Badger**—The new project you have undertaken may turn out to be harder than you expected.

**Bat**—You may have to face a crisis within your immediate family.

**Bear**—Face your burdens and your fears with courage. Your spirit helper will be at your side.

**Beaver**—Pay attention to details at home or a difficult situation will become worse.

**Bee**—You will soon receive news of an unexpected bit of good fortune.

**Boar**—Call upon the energy of your animal totem to avoid an argument with—and possible separation from—someone very close to you.

**Buffalo**—Grandmother Twylah says that to dream of a buffalo is to receive a sign that you are being given support to complete a new endeavor.

**Bull**—You will be successful in the love relationship that you have desired.

**Butterfly**—Your spirit helper may be preparing you for an act of unfaithfulness on the part of a lover.

**Cat**—Someone could be seeking your downfall or humiliation in the workplace. Ask the Great Mystery for increased awareness.

**Cock**—If you can retain control of your emotions in regard to the problem at hand, you will soon receive good news.

**Condor**—You must go into the Silence more often and receive teachings from the ancient wisdoms.

**Cougar**—An attack from an unexpected source is met successfully if you place your trust in the Great Mystery.

**Cow**—You are about to receive great financial gain.

**Coyote**—Your spirit helper may be preparing you for a death, a serious illness, or a dramatic change in your family.

**Crab**—Although the lover whose affection you desire has begun to care for you, a new rival is about to come on the scene.

**Crow**—Your animal totem is warning you that should you continue a present course of action, you will be in for a great disappointment.

**Deer**—If you continue to trust in the Great Mystery, good news and financial gain are on their way to you.

**Dog**—You may rely upon your friend to support you in a coming crisis.

**Donkey**—You must learn to control your emotions. You have been quarreling with people far too often lately.

**Dolphin**—Be prepared for a great surge of creativity.

**Dove**—Continue to maintain your peaceful attitude and a spiritual revelation may soon bring you enlightenment.

**Dragon**—Your spirit helper is warning you that certain repressed emotions may soon erupt and put you off course on your spiritual path. An unconscious desire for materialistic pleasures must be dealt with immediately.

**Duck**—You may rely upon that friend whose faithfulness you had questioned.

**Eagle**—You are facing some hard days ahead of you, but if you remember to draw upon your spiritual guidance, you will succeed.

**Falcon**—In spite of being surrounded by people who wish you to fail, your good fortune will increase.

**Fish**—If you wish that new project to succeed, you must apply yourself to it with greater seriousness.

**Fox**—Your spirit helper is advising you that you have misplaced your affections and may soon suffer a great disappointment in love.

**Frog**—You must undergo a time of cleansing in order to achieve a rebirth of your spirit.

**Gazelle**—Happiness in the form of a new lover or a new challenge is about to come into your life.

**Goat**—Do not turn your back on a potentially volatile situation in your personal relationships.

**Goose**—An inheritance is about to come to you, but you may have to travel some distance to claim it.

**Grasshopper**—Beware of danger from an unexpected source.

**Hawk**—Your new friend is completely trustworthy and has a benevolent nature.

**Horse**—You are being cautioned to continue to exercise good judgment in a current project if you wish to succeed.

**Hummingbird**—If you remain balanced, you may achieve rapid success in a new enterprise.

**Hyena**—For the next few days, do not undertake any new projects or make any important decisions after sundown.

**Jackal**—You have misjudged someone who has good intentions toward you.

**Jaguar**—You may be asked to go on an unexpected journey to a place that you have always wished to visit.

**Kangaroo**—Be very cautious in the next few days of a hostile attack from someone who has been nurturing a long-standing grudge toward you.

**Leopard**—You must seek to be more clever if you are to best a cunning adversary.

**Lizard**—You will soon receive a very profound dream teaching.

**Lion**—You have been permitting your ambitions to take on a more materialistic drive. Remember to go into the Silence and maintain balance.

**Lynx**—Your spirit helper will soon guide you to discover a secret that has long been kept from you.

**Moose**—Expect to receive a vision in which you are given an extremely potent power symbol.

**Monkey**—You have been allowing someone to make a fool of you. You must regain control of the situation.

**Mouse**—Grandmother Twylah says that to dream of a mouse is to be advised to review matters that are close at hand.

**Owl**—Pay close attention to the guidance of your spirit helper and you will avoid the snare set for you by a deceitful person whom you thought you could trust.

**Peacock**—Do not permit false pride to prevent your apologizing to the friend whose feelings you have hurt.

**Panther**—A bout of illness may be coming your way.

**Parrot**—Be on the lookout for a stranger who wishes to deceive you by flattery.

**Pigeon**—If you decide to continue your love affair, it will be successful and will lead to a happy marriage.

**Rabbit**—Stop, look, and listen! Your totem guide is telling you that you are moving too fast.

**Rat**—You need to pay closer attention to the appearance of your immediate working environment. Take some time to tidy things up a bit.

**Robin**—Someone may be about to provide you with incorrect information.

**Scorpion**—Your ideals will allow you to defeat those who oppose you.

**Seagull**—You have earned the right to feel self-satisfied over your handling of a difficult situation. Continue to remain "above things" in this regard so that you do not make the same mistake again.

**Seal**—An unexpected pregnancy will cause a great deal of emotional turmoil.

**Shark**—With the help of the Great Mystery and the strength of your animal guide, you will overcome the difficulties that have been causing you so much concern.

**Sheep**—You must become more aggressive in regard to a situation in the workplace or you will suffer the consequences of indecisiveness.

**Snake**—There are people working with you who are not what they seem. Be aware that there are deceitful people near you who talk about you behind your back.

**Spider**—Domestic problems will soon be solved, and you will soon receive great personal happiness and financial advancement.

**Stork**—There are those who are very jealous of your success. Be on guard against burglary and theft.

**Swan**—Continue to act with grace through this difficult time and you will receive a spiritual reward.

**Tiger**—If you are not mindful of details in the workplace, you may soon suffer a great embarrassment. Also, be prepared for the illness of someone very close to you.

**Turkey**—Your spirit helper is warning you against the infidelity of a lover. A series of personal calamities could cause you severe stress and bring you to the brink of nervous breakdown. Go into the Silence and receive your spiritual balance to strengthen you.

**Turtle**—If you proceed with caution and heed the advice of your spirit helper, you will succeed in the endeavor that has been troubling you.

**Unicorn**—You may receive sudden riches, but many trusted friends will turn upon you.

**Vulture**—Troubles that have been tormenting you are about to cease.

**Whale**—Although the problem may seem to be too big for you to handle, your spirit helper is reminding you that you are being guided by unseen forces of good.

**Wolf**—Be mindful that some people near you may be trying to take advantage of your trusting nature. If you heed the counsel of your spirit helper, you will achieve success in business and in love.

**Zebra**—Be aware that someone seeks to besmirch your honor and reputation.

# CHAPTER 6

# The Sacred Force Behind All Magic

Researcher-scholar Max Freedom Long contacted me in 1968 and asked if I would undertake the task of collating certain concepts of his lifelong study of the mysteries of the Kahuna, the magician-priests of Hawaii, into a single popular volume. I accepted the challenge and Max sent me package after package of books, tapes, notes, and clippings. Our correspondence through letters, and especially telephone calls, became extensive. The result of this labor of love was *Secrets of Kahuna Magic,* which was published in 1971 and remains in print twenty-six years later.

As soon as he had read the advance copy of the book that I had sent him, Max called me to say how pleased he was with the finished product. Just a very short time later, on September 23, 1971, Max Freedom Long, whom many still regard as the world's greatest authority on the Polynesian psycho-religious system known as Huna, was dead.

In this present work, in which we seek only the highest and purest methods of employing the transformative power of animal totems, we would be well-advised to review the techniques of Huna, which like all practical systems of spiritual science, employs some *unit of consciousness* guiding some *unit of force* through some *form of substance* in order to work.

The very essence of Huna lies in the belief that a human being possesses three souls: the *uhane,* a weak, animal-like spirit that speaks; the *unihipili,* a secretive spirit that sticks to, and often hides, another spirit; and the *aumakua,* the older, parental spirit, composed of both male and female elements, that has the low self (*unihipili*) and the middle self (*uhane*) under its guidance. In modern psychological terms, one might say that centuries before Freud, the Kahuna priests had discovered the conscious (*uhane*), the unconscious (*unihipili*), and the superconscious (*aumakua*).

Max had perceived the three elements which any successful system of magic must employ: a form of consciousness that directs the magical process; a force utilized by the consciousness that provides the necessary power; and a substance, visible or invisible, through which the force can act.

The *aumakua,* the High Self, is the "god" within each human. It is on this level, above the waking, conscious level, that one has the power to contact the spirit helpers, to heal, to perform miracles.

Max often told me that he had established many links between the Polynesians and the ancient Egyptians. He felt that there was a great deal of evidence to indicate that the Polynesians had left the lands in, or near, Egypt at the time prior to the "Great Drama" of Jesus, for the Hawaiians were familiar with all the principal stories in the Old Testament before the arrival of the Christian missionaries.

Max insisted that a careful study of Egyptian glyphs would reveal that they, too, were aware of the three kinds of consciousness, the three kinds of vital force (*mana*), the visible and invisible substance used by consciousness when working with the forces, and the three shadowy bodies to match the three "selves" and their three "manas."

"The glyph for spirit has always been a bird, the stork in particular," Max observed. "In early Egypt we have three storks collapsed together to make almost one, standing for the three united selves of man.

"For *mana*, the code has always been water. This glyph was not just one wavy line, but three, one above the other. And for the three shadowy bodies of man, they used three umbrellas, one for each of the three selves."

According to Huna belief, the three spirits within us are surrounded, or encased, in three shadowy bodies composed of a substance called *aka*. Each of these bodies is fed by its own supply of *mana*, the vital force. The low self (*unihipili*) utilizes simple *mana*; the middle self (*uhane*) is vitalized by a more highly charged *mana-mana*; the High Self (*aumakua*) operates on super charged *mana-loa*.

It is the role of the middle self to instruct the low self to store an extra supply of *mana* to be held in readiness for the time when it is necessary to reach up the connecting aka cord and make contact with the High Self. It is the High Self, the "god" within, that brings about the desired conditions asked in the prayer requests formed by the combined efforts of the three selves.

"*Mana* goes where it is directed and does what it is asked to do if one has full confidence so that one's low self believes that what is being done will get results," Max said. "*Mana* will travel or be projected, not only by direct physical contact (which is easiest) but along the line of sight to a person."

Max often stated that the one rule of life in Huna is that no one should do anything that might hurt another. The only sin in this spiritual philosophy is to harm another human being. To this rule, the more advanced Kahunas added loving service to their fellow humans.

Max believed he had found strong evidence that the ancient Egyptians had been equally aware of the *aka* threads.

"In some of the drawings in the tombs we see a spider pictured hanging by a thread of web above a mummy case," he explained.

"The spider was the symbol of the *aka*, or shadowy thread, at its best. In the outer teachings, it was said that one had to climb a thread of spider web to get up to heaven. The cord that goes between the physical body and the High Self is made up of many threads, thus forming a cord—the 'silver cord' mentioned in the Old Testament. In Huna, the web with the spider in the center with threads reaching out in all directions was the favorite symbol used to describe the mechanism."

In Tibet, a whole system of belief was once developed in which the universe was said to be like a web and the souls of humans were like tiny spiders dotted here and there on the vast web.

The Aborigines in Australia still have a sacred string that is a part of their personal magic kit. In Easter Island, the umbilical cord was the symbol, and such cords were carefully preserved after birth.

In the traditional Cherokee cosmology, it was the spider that answered the prayers of humans dying from bitter cold and brought the gift of fire to them on its web.

In Polynesia, Max Freedom Long noted, the word for the low self (*unihipili*) had several meanings, one of which was "sticky." This, he believed, referred to the *aka* threads, which like the web exuded by a spider, are at first sticky and will adhere to anything.

When asked why it was necessary that *mana* should be sent to the High Self when one prayed for something, Max answered in this way:

Through the silver cord, the High Self draws from the body the *mana* it ordinarily needs to live in its shadowy body. But when we ask it to make changes in our so-called dense earthly world, or the conditions in it, the secret teaching is that much more *mana* is needed, just as when we breathe more deeply to get ready to "inhale a lesson."

We accumulate the needed *mana* and send it to the High Self to use. Of the three selves, only the low self has a physical body capable of creating the life force, or *mana,* from the food, water, and air that we consume.

The prayer of the Great Drama—the life of Jesus—"Give us this day our daily bread," should read, "Let us give *you* each day *your* daily bread (*mana*)." The inward, or secret, meaning of this was lost.

In Egypt, the food of the gods, or High Selves, was symbolized by honey. Honey was secreted by the bee, so they had a sacred bee painted in the pictures in the tombs. *Mana,* when accepted by the High Self, was honey. The symbol of the High Self was light, and its symbol was the sun.

Interestingly, many cultural and spiritual traditions have made fire the symbol for revelation, inspiration, and enlightenment visited upon—or originating from—the Higher Self. Fire is also frequently used to represent the life force within each human.

Speaking from within the framework of the Shawnee belief construct, a Medicine priest once said, "Know that the life in your body and the fire on your hearth are one and the same thing, and that both proceed from the same source."

Such an observation also reminds one of the words of the great Yogi, Paramahansa Yogananda: "O Eternal Fire, Thou are shooting a little soul flame of individual human consciousness through each pore . . . of thy Universal Mind. Thou dost appear many, limited, small, divided, in these separate soul fires; but all are projections of thy One Infinite Flame."

## The Wonderful Magic of Huna Prayers

Max Freedom Long believed the central theme of Huna to be prayer and the obtaining of answers to prayers. He learned that when the Kahunas were still openly active in old Hawaii they had a ritual in which the native priest, perhaps with a chant to aid his entering a slightly altered state of consciousness, mentally gathered the aka threads from the silent worshipers who were praying for the good of the island and "braided," or united, them into a single strong strand which would reach to the High Selves who were watching.

The Kahuna then made a mental picture of the island as it should be and sent to the High Selves this image as the "seed" of the prayer to be made to grow into reality. If the prayer was performed correctly, results were expected in a rather brief period of time.

In the Huna code, the word for "braid" was *u-la-na*. The first root, *u,* is "I, myself," the same as the one used in *u-hane* for the middle self. It tells the petitioner that it is she/he who is the one to do the work of praying.

The root *la* is "light," the symbol for the High Self, which tells the petitioner to whom the prayer is to be sent.

The combined roots *la-na* mean "to float," which symbolizes the flow of *mana* along the braided cord. The stream of *mana* carries with it the thought forms of the prayer, the "seeds" of the prayer.

In Hawaiian, the word for "worship" is *ho-ano*. *Ho* is from the root "to make." *Ano* is a seed. In the Huna code we learn that the act of worship is to create a prayer "seed" to send with accumulated *mana* along the *aka* cord to the High Self.

The Hawaiian word for the answer to a prayer is *ano-hou*. Once again we find the root for "seed" and the root *hou,* which may be translated "to make new or to restore," or "to change a form or appearance."

With the meanings of *hou* emphasizing the ideas of change and restoration, Max believed that the Huna code for the answer to prayer suggested that things had been altered to conform to the prayer "seed" that had been sent to the High Self.

Since *hou* also means "to pant or to breathe heavily," we must not fail to mention the deeper breathing necessary to accumulate the *mana* necessary to carry the seed along the *aka* cord to the High Self in order to make it strong enough to answer prayers, to make the seed idea grow into tangible physical reality.

By filling our lungs and holding the breath for a few seconds, we can extract the vital force, the *mana,* to benefit our physical and spiritual well-being. To obtain the maximum physical and spiritual benefits, breathing should be rhythmic —inhalation and exhalation being of similar duration, with a short pause between the two processes. To begin, inhale for a count of twelve pulse beats, hold the breath for six, then exhale for another twelve beats. With practice, you may feel like increasing the duration of each inhalation and exhalation, but don't strain.

Among all traditional native peoples the breath is considered sacred, an agent that bestows power. In *Pueblo Gods and Myths,* Hamilton A. Tyler quotes Frank Cushing's description of a rabbit hunt in which, before an animal was completely dead, the Zuni drew the rabbit's face up to their own and "breathed from his nostrils the last faint signs of his expiring breath."

Tyler comments:

The rabbits involved were not mighty symbols, like the lion of the north, nor the spruce tree of the same direction, but lowly, indiscriminate victims of the most commonplace hunt, and yet *each one of them has a power worth preserving and incorporating into one's self.* [Italics mine]

## The Sacred Force Behind All Magic

The Kahunas of Polynesia were not alone in identifying *mana,* a remarkable force that gives energy to all miracles, prayers, healing, and acts of transcendence. All cultures at one time or another have sensed an unknown force that underlies all paranormal phenomena and which is an essential element of all life on this planet.

The Hindus call it *prana.*

The Sufis recognize it as *Baraka.*

The Chinese name it *chi.*

The Japanese identify it as *ki.*

The Old Norse blended with the energy as *wodan.*

Various Native American tribes chant its name as *wakan, manitou,* or *orenda.*

It may well be the force that in the Hebrew tradition is known as *Ruach ha-kodesh* and which the Christians welcome as the *Holy Spirit.*

Plato's *Nous* and Aristotle's Formative Cause are two other concepts that epitomize humankind's persistent attempts to identify and to define the mysterious force. Perhaps this Unknown Energy, hailed by so many names, is that same agent of which the great French Magus Eliphas Levi wrote:

> There exists an agent which is natural and divine, material and spiritual, a universal plastic mediator, a common receptacle of the vibrations of motions and the images of form, a fluid and a force, which may be called in some way the Imagination of Nature. The existence of this force is the *Great Arcanum* of practical Magick.

Throughout history, thousands of avatars, saints, healers, Shamans, gurus, Medicine priests, prophets, and miracle workers have understood that the ability to control this energy is a facet of the "god spark" within the temples of their own bodies. Unselfishly, they have tried to make all evolved and sensitive seekers of personal transformation understand that this sacred force is also accessible to them; for in some way, the human psyche serves as a conduit for this energy that, in turn, enables telepathy, psychokinesis, prophecy, clairvoyance, levitation, and so forth, to be manifested.

Shamans have claimed to be able to see the sacred energy as isolated, pulsating points of light; as spirals; or as clouds or auras surrounding the human body or an object with which a living thing has come into direct contact. When a Medicine priest projects the *mana* outward, toward others, it can be used for healing.

And what of those practitioners of the dark side of the force, those disruptive manipulators of unseen forces? Might they project the *mana* to do harm?

Proper application of the sacred energy depends upon the spiritual status and the intention of the practitioner. As long as we are on the three-dimensional, earthplane world, we must recognize the unpleasant fact that while the Unknown Energy, of itself, is neither good nor evil, like electricity, for example, it may be applied toward both positive or destructive accomplishments.

In order to isolate or define this "X-Force" somewhere within the categories of contemporary science, scientists must first begin to apprehend consciousness as a nonphysical, but very real, quality. And they must understand that physical reality is connected to consciousness by means of a single, physically fundamental, element—the sacred energy.

In this view, consciousness is more than a biochemical phenomenon confined to our bodies. Consciousness is also a force or energy that partakes of a nonphysical realm unbounded by the constraints of linear time and three-dimensional space. Therefore, mobilizing our consciousness becomes an act of psychic functioning that may impinge directly upon the universe along the entire continuum of reality—from consciousness to energy to matter. Thus, anyone capable of directing his or her consciousness with intense focus and concentration should, hypothetically, be capable of significant psychic functioning.

Science long ago discovered that everything, no matter how solid it may appear to the physical senses, is vibrating at its own particular frequency. Every human being, every animal, every band of metal, sends out shortwaves of different lengths. What is more, these personal wavelengths are as individual as fingerprints.

It has been determined that within every living organism there exists an energy, which, however weak, however unpredictable, can be refracted, polarized, focused, and combined with other energies. Sometimes it seems as though this energy has effects similar to those of magnetism, electricity, heat, and luminous radiation—yet it truly appears to be none of these things.

As one researcher told me, "I am convinced that this 'X-Force' is not related to alpha or beta particles or to gamma rays. As far as I can ascertain at this point in my research, it does not seem to fit into any part of the electromagnetic spectrum. I think it operates in an entirely different, previously unknown medium."

Paradoxically, while the Unknown Energy is often observed in the operation of heat, light, electricity, magnetism, and chemical reactions, it is somehow different from all of those known forces and energies. It appears to fill all of space, penetrating and permeating everything. Interestingly, denser materials seem to conduct it better and faster. Metal refracts it. Organic material absorbs it.

This force, sacred to true magic, unfettered by science, is basically synergetic, which means, simply stated, that it is a very cooperative energy—one that blends well with other energies. It is so cooperative that things with which it might come into contact do not disintegrate or disorganize the way they normally would.

It might be said that this energy has a basic negentropic effect, which makes it the opposite of entropy, the expected disintegration and disorganization of matter. Somehow, this mysterious force manages to violate the Second Law of Thermodynamics. It has a formative and organizing effect.

In certain experiments seeking to photograph the *mana,* the *prana,* the *ki,* around highly developed Medicine priests and devout spiritual practitioners with sensitized film, it has been found that the life-giving, synergistic energy is blue in color. On the other hand, the entropic, disintegrative energy has been photographed as yellow-red.

It has also been discovered that the synergistic energy projects a cool, pleasant feeling, while the entropic energy projects a sensation of heat and unpleasantness.

It would also appear that plants, animals, and humans contain within themselves a series of geometrical points in which the energy of the sacred force can become highly concentrated. Such points appear to be the chakras, of which the Yogis have spoken; for, in humans, these points are located at the top of the head; between the eyebrows; and in the throat, the heart, the spleen, the solar plexus, the base of the spine, and the genitals.

And as all the ancient mystery schools have told us, the sacred energy somehow flows from one living thing or from one object to another. At some level of being, the Unknown Force blends and interconnects each of us to the other—and to all living things on the planet. On some level of consciousness, every living cell is in communication with every other living cell.

Remember that the Polynesian Kahunas said that the *mana* is sticky, thereby enabling an *aka* cord, or an invisible stream of energy, to connect any two objects that have in any way been connected in the past.

Such a belief has, of course, been the very essence of sympathetic magic—a belief that one can establish nonphysical communication with, or gain information about, or do harm or healing, to someone by contact with an object previously associated with him/her.

## UNFOLDED IMAGES OF ASPECTS EXISTING IN A HIGHER REALITY

Many scientists of consciousness research have found the concept of the hologram to be a workable analogy to illustrate the Oneness of things. What is remarkable about a hologram is that every part of it contains all the information about the whole, just as the DNA in each cell of the body contains the blueprint for the entire physical structure. Split a hologram in half, shine a laser through it, and the whole object is reconstituted in three dimensions.

The human brain seems to be holographic in the manner in which it stores memory. Destroy one part of the brain and the memory survives in other parts.

Some researchers have postulated that the entire universe may be a single hologram. It may well be that information about all of it is encapsulated in each part of it. And that includes us human beings. We may all be unfolded images of aspects existing in a higher reality.

In his *Wholeness and the Implicate Order*, physicist David Bohm of the University of London raises an issue of great consequence to the subject of this book. The modern view of the world has become fragmented, Dr. Bohm states, especially in the sciences, but also in the execution of our daily lives. In orthodox science's desire to divide our universe into stars and atoms, it separated us from nature.

In humankind's prejudice of dividing itself into races, nations, political parties, and economic classes, it fragmented the individual from any underlying wholeness with others.

Dr. Bohm does not believe that it is an accident that our contemporary fragmentary form of thought is leading us to such a widespread range of crises—social, political, economic, ecological, psychological, and so forth—in the individual and in society as a whole.

As you begin more and more regularly to contact your spirit helpers, your own visions and inner teachings may soon convince you that a remarkable transformation is now taking place in all of humankind. Some turn of the great Wheel of Destiny, some advent of a new dawn on the great Cosmic Calendar, has caused the sacred force to circulate in greater strength on the Earth Mother.

Perhaps you have already awakened to the impulses of a cosmic seed within you. Perhaps you have already begun to feel the tensions and subliminal stresses as your inner guidance alerts you to a coming time of transition for the entire planet. Perhaps you have already sensed that what the spirit helpers wish most to manifest among those of us who walk the paths of the Earth Mother is balance and harmony.

Through your animal totems, you may well discover that your disciplined use of the *mana* will be of inestimable value to you in controlling virtually any environmental challenges, thus enabling you to rise above all physical considerations and to soar into higher spiritual dimensions.

# CHAPTER 7

# Praying for Strength and Guidance

S OME SCHOLARS OF ANTHROPOLOGY, mythology, and religion have speculated that all ritual observances have a distant origin, a sacred event to which a culture can trace its beginnings.

I believe that we all have our own personal myth of the beginning of our awareness of self and the cosmos, an individual sacred moment when we first had a glimpse of the true meaning of the universe, when we first felt a real connection between ourselves and other living things on Mother Earth.

My mythic beginning can be traced to those magical hours when, as a boy of three or four, I sat unseen in the midst of a clump of lilac bushes on our Iowa farm and surveyed the boundaries of my known world from the perspective of my sacred vantage point. With one arm around Bill, my big collie, connecting me with the warmth and love of a faithful animal companion, my little rump nestled in the moist, black soil of Mother Earth, I experienced the first of many epiphanies.

Today, even at the age of sixty, whenever I need help in rescuing my center from the insults of the material world, I go back in my memory to that special sacred place, my mythical moment of the beginning. Whenever I need a fortress against the stresses and pressures of the unyielding physical world, I return to my little Medicine circle in the lilac bushes. It is from this eternally secure and sheltered vantage spot that I can regroup my spiritual and physical energies, shore up my mental faculties, and resume the quest with renewed strength and guidance.

I believe that you also have a similar magic place—a sacred spot to which you retreated as a child and felt secure and protected against the fears and threats of an outside world that seemed alien to your essential self and your inner spark of divinity. I believe that you, too, have a personal myth of your beginning of awareness on Mother Earth.

## THE MEDICINE WHEEL—
## A SPIRITUAL SENDING AND RECEIVING STATION

Although most of us cannot physically return to the place of our personal mythic origins—my lilac bushes are long gone—we can reclaim our spiritual innocence and empower our prayers to the Great Mystery by centering ourselves in the Medicine Wheel.

I think I was about thirteen when I first heard about the great Medicine Wheel in the Big Horn Mountains of Wyoming. This mother of all Medicine Wheels forms an almost perfect circle 70 feet in diameter and 245 feet in circumference. Its "hub" is twelve feet in diameter with a seven-foot opening in its middle. Twenty-eight stone "spokes" reach out from the axis to the outer rim of the wheel. Six large monuments are located around the rim, and other monuments have been built on high points of land at some distance from the wheel.

To this day, no one knows who built the wheel, not even the tribes who once inhabited the area. There are a lot of educated guesses, but no definitive answer.

A well-informed Shoshone, who devoted a great deal of time to studying the history of his people, said that it had to be of prehistoric origin. "Our people say it was there long before our fathers came to the land," he said. "The Crows believed that the wheel was the work of the Great Mystery, who dropped it down from the sky."

Certain archaeologists have pointed out that the wheel is not unlike the strange religious megalithic rims built by forgotten early Europeans. Others have noted its curious similarity to the great ceremonial calendar wheels constructed in Mexico by the Aztecs.

There are some authorities who have fixed the date of the wheel's construction all the way from 15,000 to 1,000 B.C.E. And there is a general consensus that whoever built the Medicine Wheel, it was no known Native American tribe. While the Big Horn Mountains held great spiritual significance for the tribes in the area—the Crow, Sioux, Araphao, Shoshone, and Cheyenne—none of them ever constructed anything of stone—not houses, not forts, not temples, not even gravestones.

"It is sacred to us because it is older than the memory of our tribe," a Medicine practitioner from the Crow told me. "I believe that the Star Beings built it to remind us always of the power of the Great Mystery."


## BUILD YOUR OWN MEDICINE WHEEL

Among contemporary Native Americans, the Medicine Wheel is considered a place for spiritual communion wherever it is constructed. And since there is no one set, dogmatic layout to the wheel, it lends itself perfectly to individual or group prayers for strength and guidance.

Here is the way that some friends and I constructed a Medicine Wheel in a large clearing in a wooded area. You may follow this layout to create your own spiritual sending and receiving device to the Great Mystery.

Begin with the center stone. In our wheel, this was Turtle, to represent the way of peace.

Around the center stone, place seven smaller stones in a circle. These stones stand for the seven colors of the rainbow, the seven notes of the scale, the seven days of the week, and so forth. The numbers seven and four are sacred to most Native American tribes.

The four stones of the spirit keepers should be placed equidistant from the center stone in the four directions. How far you set them depends, of course, on the dimensions of the Medicine Wheel that you are constructing. Our wheel placed the Frog in the north, the Dog in the south, the Owl in the east, and the Wolf in the west.

The four "spokes" of the wheel generally consist of three stones in each of the four directions, spaced as equidistantly as possible. Some Medicine practitioners use red stones for the north-south path and black stones for east-west. As I said previously, there is no dogma in building the Medicine Wheel, so use whatever rocks are accessible to you.

Regardless of the color of the rocks, however, you might wish to observe a tradition that sees the southern path as that of trust and love on the earthwalk; the northern path as that of cleansing and renewal; the western path as that of self-examination; and the eastern path as that of wisdom and enlightenment.

The twelve moon (month) stones are the last to be set in place. Various tribes had different names for the months, so you may either do a little research before you begin construction on your wheel and adopt the naming system of a tribe with whom you feel some identification, or you may use the names from our circle.

Beginning with Wolf in the west and moving north toward Frog, place the first stone, the Traveling Moon (October); then the Beaver Moon (November); and third, the Hunting Moon (December).

Placing stones from north (Frog) to east (Owl), the Cold Moon (January); the Snowy Moon (February); and the Green Moon (March).

Placing stones from east (Owl) to south (Dog), the Moon of Plants (April); the Moon of Flowers (May); and the Hot Moon (June).

Placing stones from south (Dog) to west (Wolf), the Moon of the Deer (July); the Sturgeon Moon (August); and the Fruit Moon (September).

Now the Medicine Wheel is complete. You now have your own microcosm, your own daughter of the Earth Mother. This can be your personal place of prayer, meditation, vision, revelation, enlightenment. You may share it with your friends, with groups of spiritual seekers, or maintain it as your own private outdoor chapel.

## RECEIVING MEDICINE WHEEL VISIONS AND PRAYERS

One of the primary aspects of Native American Medicine Power is a strong belief in the partnership between the world of the physical and the world of spirit. If you begin your use of the Medicine Wheel out of a sense of levity, you are indicating your desire to fail at a most vital and serious project. Some supplicants achieve amazing results in a relatively short period of time. For others, the development of spiritual empowerment may take weeks or months.

At the beginning, take whatever may come to you, regardless of how small or seemingly irrelevant the manifestations or messages may seem. Keep at it. Wait for better results. They will come if your perseverance and patience remain strong.

As much as possible, set a regular time for your development exercises at the Medicine Wheel. Don't overdo it by becoming a slave to the clock or by sitting, standing, or dancing too often. At the beginning it might be best for you to choose a power place that feels right to you in the wheel and assume a comfortable position either sitting or lying down. Later, when you have truly begun to feel in tune with the wheel's vibration, you can add drumming, singing, and dancing.

The time of day most suitable for your training and experimentation with the Medicine Wheel is either the latter part of the day or early evening, when you are finished with the day's responsibilities; or at sunrise, before you have assumed the frantic pace of work and family concerns.

Sit quietly. Divest your thoughts of your immediate worldly challenges and attempt to keep your mind blank.

Place yourself in as receptive a mood as possible. Be alert, but don't expect anything in particular to occur. Be patient and wait.

Once you have worked with the Medicine Wheel for quite some time, you may conduct solitary sittings and meditations in complete confidence. At the beginning of your experimentation it is best to work with one or more other persons. Not only does the presence of others considerably lessen the danger of fatigue or boredom, but it is undeniable that two or three people, even during the period of preliminary training, can accomplish more than the single experimenter. You must be certain, however, that you pick like-minded individuals to participate in your sessions.

For obvious reasons, you would not be likely to ask any friends who are hard-nosed skeptics and materialists to join you. Nor would you be wise in inviting "true believers" who would see a profound manifestation of the supernatural in every warble of a meadowlark. It would be most desirable to choose friends who are interested in spiritual development and the use of animal totems, who have a good deal of patience, and who give evidence of a rather well-established sense of balance between the physical and the nonphysical.

If genuine phenomena such as points of light darting about or the fleeting appearance of animal or human spirit forms should begin to manifest even during your first sitting, don't be surprised and don't be frightened. Such signs are merely indications that you are well on your way to developing spiritual strength. Wait patiently for what may happen next. Don't expect immediate miracles and don't be overly critical of what may manifest during those early sittings.

In order to raise the vibratory level of your Medicine Wheel, you may like to drum for a while. Some of the members of your group may feel the urge to sing or to chant. Others may wish to bring fetishes, images of their animal totems, to encourage the manifestation of the spirit helpers.

When spirit manifestations begin, welcome the entities warmly. Speak to them confidently and calmly. When contact is firmly established, it will be possible to communicate with your spirit helpers telepathically—and sometimes, as your talents progress, orally. Almost certainly, results will get better and better and gain in importance from sitting to sitting.

The messages you receive may vary greatly in value and content. Sometimes they may be startling, sometimes somewhat trivial, and other times couched in highly symbolic language. Your seriousness and your openness to receive meaningful communication will in large part determine the quality of the messages that you receive.

Do not be concerned if you should enter the trance state during certain of your sittings. Trance is a completely natural and normal state that occurs in psychically gifted persons in order to facilitate their communication with the world of spirit.

Since entranced people remember little or nothing of what takes place or what they may say, it is important that you or another member of your circle have a tape recorder ready to make a record of the messages received from the entranced subject. Memory should not be relied upon.

## A Vision of Two Shamans from Spirit Time

One day, just at sunset, I found my power place in the Medicine Wheel that we constructed. It felt best to me to sit next to Wolf, my principal totem animal.

A large part of our motivation in constructing the Medicine Wheel was to be able to use it as an energizer for prayer and meditation, so I offered up a prayer to the Great Mystery, giving thanks for the wonder and beauty of the Earth Mother. I began to focus on the center stone, the one that we had dedicated to Turtle, the peacemaker. I thought of Grandmother Twylah, who had received a revelation of a process that she called the Pathway of Peace.

And then I became aware of the image of a Shaman standing in the Medicine Wheel with a crow on his left shoulder and a hawk on his right shoulder. My inner being reminded me that many Native American tribes regard birds as messengers of the Great Mystery. As the winged ones soared to the clouds, one might easily imagine that they were carrying prayers from the two-leggeds on earth to the Great Mystery above.

When the Shaman lifted his arms, I saw a most peculiar thing. Instead of his arms ending in hands, they had been transformed into colorful birds, very much resembling parrots. I understood that he was showing me in symbolic form that he was a prophet. The brightly colored birds relayed prophecies to him, one for each ear. It was apparent that the Shaman must always exercise great caution in issuing his predictions, for with a bird chattering into each ear, it would be easy to become confused with so much cross-communication.

The Shaman waved his unusual appendages before his chest, and they once again became conventional hands with five fingers each instead of beaks and feathers. His sudden movement caused the crow, another of my totem animals, to fly from his shoulder. The crow gave a series of calls, and suddenly an aspect of myself was flying with him.

At first I could clearly see the Medicine Wheel in the field below, and then it became apparent that we were soaring into another dimension of time and space. It seemed as though I was seeing strange memory patterns flickering in my consciousness. I wasn't certain if they were my memories or those of another, but it didn't really seem to matter.

I was now standing in an ancient city made of stone high in the mountains. I had an inner knowing of the Andes mountains in Peru. And though I had not yet traveled there in my physical body, I very much felt that I was standing in Machu Piccu when it was a thriving city.

The memories that I perceived were those of a student of a most special teacher, a High Priest, who stood before me now in a brilliantly colorful robe that seemed to have been fashioned from the feathers of a hundred different birds.

I was being told by an inner awareness that this High Priest, this master teacher, had made me his prize pupil. I, more than any of the other initiates, had responded perfectly to his teachings. When the great teacher made a particular sound on the vessel that he held in his hand, I was able to leave my body and soar free of my physical limitations. I could move free of time and space. I could go anywhere that I wished in an instant. Once I was free of the body, I had but to think of a destination and I could be there.

And, then, in a dreamlike state, I saw myself walking down a path surrounded by the master teacher's other students. I am proud that I have been selected for this very special demonstration.

It is night. There is a full moon. We are walking to the main altar of the city. As I look around at the students and the members of a crowd that has formed, it seems as though I recognize some of the faces—their eyes especially.

We approach the place where the demonstration is to be held, and I see a large, rectangular stone that juts out of a clearing before the principal altar. My teacher, the High Priest, is already there. His multicolored, feathered cloak is blowing open in a gentle breeze. On either side of him stands a priest of lower rank.

A dozen or so students step forward from the crowd and spread a blanket on the rock for me. I move into the circle and lie down on the coarse cloth blanket. I take a deep breath and look up at the full moon. A small cloud moves across its face. I lie quietly for a few moments, then indicate to the High Priest that I am ready.

I am calm. I am relaxed. And then I hear the High Priest blowing on the vessel and producing a strange sound that seems immediately to begin to tug at my spirit. I know that I have been conditioned, programmed, to respond to that sound from the vessel. I know that within moments, the real me will burst free of the limitations of the physical body and shoot up to the clouds, toward the moon.

And then I feel myself rushing, pushing, pulsating, spinning, and breaking free of the bonds of flesh and bone. The real me soars toward the moon. The universe is now only my spirit and the Great Mystery. I am free of time and space.

I knew that I was supposed to return with specific information to prove that my out-of-body flight was successful, but I was suddenly sitting back beside Wolf rock in the Medicine Wheel. I hoped that the student in that alternate reality returned to his teacher and proved the demonstration a complete success.

I was left with the momentary dilemma of deciding which scenario was my true reality. The Shaman in the Medicine Wheel was gone, but I knew that the rocks in the spokes and rim were real, the grass was real.

However, I had to ask myself, was the rock from which I launched my demonstration in the ancient city—and the ancient city and its inhabitants—any less real?

## GRANDMOTHER TWYLAH'S PATHWAY OF PEACE

Grandmother Twylah of the Seneca has a beautiful ritual that she calls the Pathway of Peace, which she first shared with me in 1972. This pathway utilizes seven stones, emphasizing the number so sacred to most Native American tribes. The revelation of the ceremony began when Twylah received the following message after spending three days in the Silence:

> The Pathway of Peace leads toward peace of mind
> The sharing of gifts to every kind
> Of creation living upon this earth,
> Measuring the steps of each one's worth.
> Seek the trail of Seven Stones
> Where Spiritual songs of harmonic tones
> Fill the world in harmony,
> Soothing throngs of creatures into serenity.
> Desire peaks into the soul
> Where gifts of life are there to behold
> Where charms of peace and harmony
> Belong to all for eternity.

Briefly summarizing the inspiring process of enlightenment that constitutes the Pathway of Peace, the first stepping stone as seen clearly in Twylah's vision was the Blood-stone, glowing in radiant shades of red. The purpose of this stone is to beckon the seekers to the Pathway of Peace and to awaken within them the seed of faith in the spiritual way of life.

The Blood-stone has seven facets, each one designating one of the spiritual senses of sound, sight, scent, taste, touch, awareness, and emotions. When the supplicants stand on the first stone, it is symbolic of the life materialized in the physical world, a daily venture in faith.

As the radiance of the Blood-stone flows through the spiritual seekers, they learn that the Great Mystery, the Spiritual Essence, is connected with all things in creation and that all things in creation are connected with one another.

The second stepping stone in Twylah's vision of the Pathway of Peace is the Sun-stone, which glows in radiant shades of yellow and plants the seed that awakens the supplicants to the spiritual way of love.

The seven facets of the Sun-stone are the same seven spiritual senses, but to stand on this stone is symbolic of a daily venture of love.

As the radiance of the Sun-stone flows through the supplicants, they learn that it is the spiritual expression of faith and love that makes the world go around and enables all seekers to grown in peace and harmony.

The third stepping stone, the Water-stone, glows in radiant shades of blue and plants the seed that awakens the supplicants to the spiritual way of cleansing and soothing.

The seven facets of the Water-stone are once again the seven spiritual senses, but to stand on the stone is symbolic of the daily venture of cleansing.

As the radiance of the Water-stone flows through the supplicants, they learn that it is the fluid property that unites all creation into the stream of spirituality and helps them grow toward peaceful relaxation.

The fourth stepping stone, the Fertility-stone, glows in radiant shades of green and awakens the seed that alerts the supplicants to the spiritual way of abundance and renewal.

The seven sides of the Fertility-stone also designate the seven spiritual senses, but to stand on the stone is symbolic of a daily venture in physical and natural growth.

As the radiance of the Fertility-stone flows through the supplicants, they learn that environmental awareness will help them grow toward peace and harmony with all creation.

The fifth stepping stone, the Blossoming-stone, glows in radiant shades of coral pink and awakens the seed that causes the supplicants to dwell upon the spiritual way of upliftment.

The seven sides of the Blossoming-stone have the same powerful facets as the previous stones, but to stand on the stone is symbolic of the daily venture in intuitive impulses.

As the radiance of the Blossoming-stone flows through the supplicants, they learn to nourish the material world with beauty and spiritual insight.

The sixth stepping stone, the Charity-stone, glows in a radiant burst of spiritual light and awakens the seed that beckons the supplicants to the spiritual way of benevolence in thoughts and deeds.

The Charity-stone has the same powerful seven facets, but to stand on the stone is symbolic of nourishing the material world with acts of kindness and understanding.

As the radiance of the Charity-stone flows through the suppli-cants, they become united with all creation in the ways of spiritual harmony.

The seventh stepping stone, the Healing-stone, glows in radiant shades of lavender, and it awakens the supplicants to the way of spir-itual healing—the highest creative spirituality.

The Healing-stone has the same seven powerful facets, but to stand on the stone is symbolic of the spiritual attunement that flows throughout Eternity.

As the radiance of the Healing-stone flows through the suppli-cants, they become aware that they stand at the threshold of the Great Silence that opens the way of Spiritual Peace and Harmony.

> In the Silence
> All creation unites and communicates
> The Spiritual Way.
> Where life is pure, life is fulfilling;
> Life is understanding; life is sharing;
> Life is abundant; life is unity; and
> Life is Eternity.
> The ecstasy of Spiritual Enlightenment.
> As the seeker descends the Pathway of Peace—
> The seventh stepping stone reveals Spiritual Healing.
> The sixth stepping stone reveals Spiritual Charity.
> The fifth stepping stone reveals Spiritual Insight.
> The fourth stepping stone reveals Spiritual Awareness.
> The third stepping stone reveals Spiritual Cleansing.
> The second stepping stone reveals Spiritual Love.
> The first stepping stone reveals the Spiritual Path.
> The Light of all Light,
> The Light of all Faith and Love,
> The Light of all Knowledge and Inspiration,
> The Source of all Creation—
> The Spiritual Revelation.

## How Animal Totems Deliver Answers to Prayers

To illustrate further that an awareness of one's animal totems need not conflict in any way with what some folks might term their more orthodox or conventional religious beliefs, I present the thoughts and experiences of Beverly Hale Watson, who gained her reputation as an author primarily in the area of inspirational works written from a biblical perspective. However, being the curious person that she is, Beverly says, "The Lord opened a number of doors so I could meet with some traditional Native Americans and discuss their beliefs." Since her exposure to various tribal cultures, Beverly says that God has sent many animals to her.

"Birds, however, seem to be the most frequent. Hawks seem to be constantly nearby. Once I even had birds show up late at night in answer to prayer. These birds were small and bedecked in colors that I had never seen before. I'll admit that I don't understand all of these things, but I can definitely attest to the fact that focusing on the Creator for answers can change your life."

Beverly tells of a mystical experience that occurred when she and her husband, Paul, were touring some ancient ruins near Sedona, Arizona.

"I was led to an egg-shaped rock conclave that faced the mountainside. Spirit told me that I was to crawl inside and begin toning various sounds that would be given to me. When the sounds came through, ancient Amerindian symbol writing appeared on the wall in front of me.

"Spirit next told me to leave that spot and to go to the rim of the mountain which overlooked the valley below. There more sounds would be given to me. Spirit also said that the five people who were with me were to repeat the sounds as they came to me.

"As we followed Spirit's instructions, to our left, along the mountain wall, more symbol writing appeared—together with the spirit forms of Indians dressed in full tribal regalia. These manifestations were visible to all six of us.

"Then a flock of birds formed in the middle of the valley below and rose to circle a tree in front of us. When I realized that this was a sign from Spirit, they flew into a single file, moved off into the

distance, went around the mountain edge to our right, and disappeared."

In her office in their home in Charlotte, North Carolina, Beverly
Hale Watson has a large window that provides her with an excellent
view of the woods surrounding their house.

"Often I find myself staring outside, awaiting that inspirational
thought when I am composing a story," she says. "On this one particular Saturday, the sentences were flowing faster than I could peck
them out on the computer keyboard. Suddenly the shrill call of a
hawk pierced the silence and totally disrupted my concentration."

Beverly spotted the hawk gracefully soaring above the trees, the
unsettling sound of its screeching cry intensifying as the large bird
neared their house. Seconds later, the hawk glided to a halt, grasping
a tree branch directly outside her office window. It was as if it had
selected the perfect vantage point from which to observe her at
work.

"Perched in a stately manner on the limb, the hawk stood about
eighteen inches high," Beverly says. "Our eyes connected immediately, and I had an inner sense that this bird was somehow different."

After thirty minutes of intense observation and unrelenting eye
contact with the hawk, Beverly decided to go back to her writing.
Out of the corner of her eye, she could see the large bird watching
her as she typed.

"The hawk never budged. His eyes were continually focused on
what I was doing. He watched my every move for exactly two hours
and fifty-five minutes!"

This incident aroused such a curiosity within her about the interrelationship between humans and the animal kingdom that Beverly
decided she must learn more about Native American culture. Earlier
in her quest for wisdom, she had met a Medicine man who had become one of her mentors. When she contacted him and told him of
the strange experience with the hawk, he explained that the hawk,
the Messenger of the Sky, was her totem animal.

"The hawk would be akin to Mercury, the messenger of the gods,"
Beverly says. "Since I pen spiritually inspired books, I thought it
most fitting that the hawk would be my totem animal."

Since her first hawk encounter many years ago, Beverly says that rarely a day goes by in which at least one of the magnificent birds does not appear to her.

"In the summertime, it isn't uncommon to see three hawks circling over my head as I work in the garden. They will screech loudly as they approach our property, giving me just enough time to look upward as they fly by. Many times they soar over me as I am headed down our long driveway to the mailbox.

"On numerous occasions when traveling by automobile, hawks soar in front of me, as if leading the way. For years now, I have taken delight in counting the number of hawks that perch beside the road when we travel."

On a recent two-and-a-half-hour trip, Beverly says that she counted a total of twenty-nine hawks. "And some of our constant companions skimmed the roof of our car."

On that same trip, just prior to leaving their cabin, which was situated near a sacred Cherokee site, she received a message from Spirit to take her drum and to go outside and sit quietly at the picnic table. Once she and her companion had followed those instructions, beautiful Native American songs would be sung through them.

"We did as told, and beautiful chants began to flow from our mouths. Our hands automatically began producing rhythms on the drum in perfect synchronicity with the songs."

Within minutes, Beverly says, a crow could be heard vocalizing its caw-caw. It flew to a tree within five feet of them. Cocking its head, listening to the sounds, the crow flapped its wings to perch on a low limb just above their heads.

"It soon began to sing with us. A second crow followed the course of the first one, resting on a branch in front of us. Shortly thereafter, a large assortment of smaller birds joined our chorus—each voice and each melody blending with the others to create the most beautiful harmonics. The two of us sat in awe as we sang totally unfamiliar songs, wondrously accompanied by our feathered friends. The experience will definitely be long remembered!"

Beverly Hale Watson also told me of numerous occasions when her totem animal appeared in answer to prayer.

During a recent ice storm, the Watsons were left without any electricity or heat for four days. The temperatures had dropped into the single digits, thus challenging them to be creative when it came to keeping warm.

"We spent four days bundled up in layered clothing, then sliding under several blankets. When the sun appeared over the horizon and streamed in our glass windows and doors, we hurried to absorb as much of the warmth of its rays as we could. Not knowing how many more days we could physically withstand the cold temperatures, I prayed for a sign that help was on its way. Three minutes before our electricity was restored, a large red-tailed hawk flew in front of the window, his cry signaling that our plea had been heard."

Beverly testifies that when she has least expected it, God, the Great Spirit, has given her glimpses of His omnipotent power. And the hawk has been His messenger.

"The past two years, three of these birds have been regular residents on our property. One pair has a nest in a nearby tree, and each spring they return to it. While these birds appear to be physically solid, we have had other hawks literally materialize out of nowhere, circle us, then disappear before our eyes."

This reminded Beverly of an incident that had occurred on Bald Head Island. Bald Head Island is a small vacation hideaway off the coast of North Carolina that can be accessed only by boat. Once one arrives on the island, transportation is achieved only by bicycle, golf cart, or foot.

"Our host was a resident of the island," Beverly says, "very familiar with the alligator habitats and the winding cart paths. My husband and I, plus seven other individuals who also work with gifts of the Holy Spirit, had come together for a meeting.

"After settling in at our lodging site, we received information from the Inner Voice that we were to be on the beach at midnight. Upon our arrival, Divine Guidance was given as to exactly where we were to sit in a circle. Each person had a piece of the puzzle in terms of information that had been conveyed."

After prayer and meditation, as the session was coming to a close, Beverly asked that the Holy Spirit give them a sign of its presence.

"Within minutes, a shadow of a huge bird could be seen flying above the ocean toward us. As it approached, its features became more distinct. It resembled an eagle with a wing span of several feet. None of us could believe what we were seeing!

"As the huge bird reached the beach area, it suddenly made a U-turn directly over our heads. As it headed back out to the ocean, it literally vanished into thin air. All of us sat speechless."

Beverly has since learned that Eagle Medicine is the power of the Great Spirit, a connection to the Divine.

"We have the ability to live in the realm of spirit, but we must also remain connected and balanced within the Earth realm. This incident proved to us that although wisdom can manifest in many strange and curious forms, it is always related to the creative force of God, the Great Spirit."

Beverly has no doubt that her totem animal is the hawk.

"I view him as a messenger sent from God as a symbol that I am never alone. A perfect example of this occurred when I recently completed a five-month assignment doing the Lord's work. My office was located in a building in downtown Charlotte. As I exited the premises for the last time, circling in front of the building, approximately eight feet from the ground, was a hawk. At that precise moment, I heard the Voiceless Voice say, 'A job well done!' I blinked my eyes, and the hawk was gone."

Beverly has always respected the wide variety of birds, fish, animals, and plants in God's Kingdom. "Each is unique in design and characteristics. When humankind truly understands that *all* is of one, they will discover the beauty of living in harmony.

"All of God's creations are infused with the Spirit of Life. Recognizing that Spirit within all living things can create an invisible bonding that will truly surpass all understanding. People have many things in common with animals. By studying their nature, traits, habits, and movements, one can ascertain the 'medicine' that they are trying to teach us."

# CHAPTER 8

# Avoiding the Horrid Things of Darkness

Aᴌᴛʜᴏᴜɢʜ ᴛʜᴇ ʙᴇʟɪᴇꜰ ɪɴ a personal devil is common in many of the religious concepts of humankind, the traditional Native Americans did not conceive of an omnipresent evil spirit that had been created by the Great Mystery for the purpose of tempting humans into sin or damnation. A legend among certain of the eastern tribes, however, explains the evil spirit as a mistake of the Creator Spirit—which is perhaps as wise a way of dealing with the perplexing question of the origin of evil as that taken by many philosophers and theologians.

According to this legend, the Great Creator Spirit was enjoying himself fashioning all the many animals out of cakes of clay when he rather whimsically began to toy around with a very large creature. He bestowed on it sure feet and claws like that of the panther; strong and broad shoulders like that of the buffalo; scales like those of the alligator; eyes like those of the lobster; a nose like the beak of the vulture; a tuft of porcupine quills for a scalp-lock; gills like the fish; wings like those of a giant bat; long, sharp teeth set in the mouth of the lizard; and the forked tongue of the snake.

Although the Creator of Life had sought to amuse himself with such a monstrous being, it terrified all the other animals and caused the spirit beings to be very apprehensive. And, then, before the Great Mystery could think better of his grotesquerie and remove the spark of life from the hideous beast, it ran away to begin a reign of terror wherever it wandered.

It was only then that the Great Mystery realized that a mistake had been made. The forests, skies, grasses, and waters of the paradise on Turtle Island were now fouled by his inadvertent creation of the Evil Spirit.

## FACING THE DARK SIDE WITH DISCERNMENT, DISCIPLINE, AND DIRECT ACTION

Confronting evil and negativity is a large part of walking in balance on the Earth Mother. One cannot hide from evil, and one certainly cannot ignore it. The Dark Side of the Force must be faced with discernment, discipline, and direct action.

In his lifelong study of the Huna system, Max Freedom Long warned others that there truly are horrid things that belong in the realm of darkness. "We moderns are powerless to combat them," he observed, "because we have become too civilized to realize that they are there. Doctors know nothing of them. Priests and ministers have such a garbled idea of devils that their advice is useless."

In Max's opinion, among the priceless gifts which the Kahuna priests have given to the world is a clear and comprehensive knowledge of the horrid things of darkness and an effective way of fighting them.

From the Huna perspective, the basic troublemakers are the low selves that get separated from their middle selves after a person's death. These entities may then become the poltergeists, the noisy, furniture-tossing "ghosts" that haunt homes and molest the living. These rampant low selves are without the ability to reason, for they have lost contact with their middle selves and have become the spirits that obsess the living and sometimes render the particularly vulnerable insane.

For the most part, the Kahunas hold that these low selves are fairly harmless, but because they may in many cases steal *mana* from the living, they can solidify their shadowy bodies sufficiently to enable them to move physical objects. And it must always be understood that these entities have the potential to become the "vampires" that prey upon the living, stealing enough of their vital force to cause complete exhaustion or mysterious death.

In other situations, these predatory low selves may attach themselves to humans, thus becoming parasite personalities and causing obsession, erratic behavior, crime, vile acts, and insanity. To the tormented mind of the victim, these invading entities may appear as grotesque animal-like demons with fangs and claws.

In Huna, possessing entities are called "eating companions," for they hover around certain individuals and "eat" their *mana* in order to make themselves strong. At the same time, they exert a hypnotic influence over the victims and cause them to do various things against their will.

In advanced cases of this type of low self possession, the tormented victim can come to believe that he himself is a vampire or a werewolf; and just as the invading, parasitic low self is slowly eating him alive by stealing his life force, so does his confused mind believe that he must literally eat other humans to preserve his own existence.

## How to Protect Yourself from Evil Spirits

I have often discussed with Shamans and Medicine priests from many different disciplines and tribes the matter of lower-plane spirits who seek to possess the physical bodies of humans. I am presenting now certain warnings, admonitions, and methods of protection that seemed to surface repeatedly in my analyses of over thirty years of conferences on "evil spirits."

1. Discordant spirits cannot achieve power over a human unless they are somehow invited into a person's private space—or unless they are attracted to a human aura that emanates negativity.

2. Discordant or low-self entities are parasites of the soul that crave to continue to experience the pleasures of the flesh that they so enjoyed when they were in human bodies. For this reason, they are always seeking physical shells to inhabit in order to perpetuate their desires.

3. Humans are especially susceptible to such spirit invasion when they are exploiting one another sexually or when they have abused alcohol or drugs and their normal boundaries of control have been removed.

4. Never enter meditation or initiate contact with your totem animal with the sole thought of obtaining personal satisfaction or ego aggrandizement. Selfish motivation may risk your becoming easily affected by those spirits who have been entrapped in a hellish domain of their own making.

5. Whenever you engage in any spiritual exercise or technique, envision a Golden Circle of Protection completely encircling you. Ask the Great Mystery and your spirit helper to keep watch so that you interact only with those entities of the most loving and harmonious vibrations.

6. When seeking contact with your spirit helper, remember always that our physical reality is closer to the realm of the lower, more chaotic, frequencies, than it is to the dimension of the most harmonious. Because we exist in a material world, the efforts of our psyches will always contain more of the lower vibratory realm than the higher planes.

7. Prepare yourself for communication with your animal totem by bathing yourself in a wondrous expression of unconditional love.

8. Be aware that if you should meet a being from the lower, chaotic realms, masquerading as your spirit helper, you will

feel at once a prickling sensation that will seem to crawl over your entire body. You will instantly be filled with doubt. You will experience a mounting sensation of unease, depending upon the strength of the discordant vibrations emanating from the deceitful spirit being.

If you should encounter such a chaotic being, utter prayers and blessings of love at once. Fill your entire essence with unconditional love for all of the Great Mystery's creations—and firmly, free of fear, reject the advances of the discordant entity.

9. In order to prevent contact with negative, low-self entities, you must practice equally and unconditionally loving all creatures formed by the Great Mystery; and you must seek to elevate the consciousness of all humankind by your thoughts, words, and deeds. Keep your purpose on the level of highest vibration, and you will only receive meaningful, inspirational contact with your spirit helper.

10. Understand that evil or negativity is an imbalance, a chaotic, ignorant, mindless energy or vibration. It is a destructive energy, the opposite of growth and productivity.

When you are negative, depressed, angry, or jealous, you place yourself "on target" for the chaotic, mindless, destructive vibration that comes from the dimension of the lesser energies, the lower frequencies.

11. Never forget that all that exists vibrates at its own particular frequency, at its own energy level. By going into the Silence, focusing upon the strength of the Great Mystery, and calling upon your spirit helper, you can develop the power and the ability to raise your vibrational frequency.

## TRANSFORMING NEGATIVITY

If you should sense the presence of discordant entities in your environment, practice this exercise:

Bend your elbows and lift your hands, palms outward to the level of your chest. Take a comfortably deep breath, then emit the universal sound of "OM" in a long drawn-out chant: "O-O-O–O-M-M-M."

Repeat this until you are able to feel the energy tingling the palms of your hands. Once you feel more positive, bring your palms toward each other until you feel the *mana*, the Life Force, as a palpable "substance" between them. Focus on this energy.

Visualize the energy moving upward from your palms to your fingers. Feel it moving up your arms, your shoulders, your neck, your face. See the energy feeding new life, new *mana*, to your entire physical being.

Utter the universal sound of "OM" once again. Visualize your totem guide joining you, standing nearby to offer strength and protection. With the added energy of your spirit helper near you, see the energy moving up to the top of your head, then cascading down in sparks of golden light, as if you were being enveloped by the downward outpouring of a roman candle. Impress upon your consciousness that those "sparks" represent new, positive energy that is descending around your physical body and your spirit to form a vital protective shield against discordant and disruptive entities.

## MAKING YOUR OWN MEDICINE SHIELD

For some time now I have been making Medicine Shields to serve as a barrier against any negative energies that seek to disrupt our home environment. Each shield is individually crafted and centered around the theme of spiritual protection. No two shields are exactly alike, but each one is infused with the energies of love, light, and healing—together with the spirit of Oneness in the Great Mystery and respect toward all lifeforms on the Earth Mother.

The Medicine Shield is placed on a wall, set on a bookshelf, hung in an automobile, or situated wherever I feel it is most needed to protect my wife, Sherry, and me from the stresses and trials that must be faced in seeking to walk a path of balance.

I can also use my Medicine Shield as a mandala in meditative contemplation during my quiet time. Each object on the shield may serve as a focus for inner exploration as I reflect on the deeper meaning of the symbolic interplay.

Let me describe a shield that I have at hand. I have taken a piece of leather, roughly triangular in shape, approximately thirteen inches at the base, eleven inches on the sides. I have left the leather its natural color of reddish brown, but I have painted a large blue center with a smaller white circle inside. Within the white circle, I have drawn a Native American glyph which represents a thunder being.

At the top of the rough triangle, I have cemented a small ceramic turtle totem image. At the bottom right, I have fixed a small ceramic bear totem image. Sherry utilizes her Chippewa heritage and her artistic talent to cast these from impressions in sand.

Just above the bear image, I have cemented an almost perfectly shaped round white stone which I found in a sacred area. In the center of the shield, I have attached a piece of coral from a South Pacific island. On the left edge of the shield I have placed two small sea shells from the beach near a sacred teacher's garden. On each of the bottom sides I have hung a leather thong decorated with small beads and bells. Each of the various stones, bells, beads, shells, or other objects have been given to Sherry and myself as we have traveled to sacred Medicine areas and holy sites throughout the world.

To create your own Medicine Shield, obtain a piece of leather and select your own sacred objects to cement in place on its surface. Go into the Silence to decide which totem animals you wish to place on the shield and to determine which of your holy objects should accompany them. Refer to the Totem Animal Dictionary on page 151 to assist you in choosing spirit helpers that convey the symbols of empowerment that you would like to place on your Medicine Shield.

If you cannot find or make images of your totem animals to cement on your shield, paint their likenesses on the leather surface to the best of your ability. Remember, this is your personal shield of protection from negative entities. You are designing it for your own peace of mind, not to hang it in an art gallery for others to appraise.


## SUMMONING YOUR SPIRIT HELPER TO BANISH EVIL

I know a number of Medicine practitioners who at all times carry in their spirit bag a crystal by which they summon their totem guide to assist them in banishing evil. For this exercise you must understand that by focusing the violet light of transmutation through your crystal, your spirit helper can banish all negativity from your life.

The violet light is the highest vibratory level in the spectrum of light vibration. By calling upon your totem guide to focus the violet light, you can balance the negativity that you may have sown or that you may have directed against yourself. Know and understand that you, under the direction of your spirit helper, may use the violet light in a daily ritual of transmutation, thus removing all negativity and fear from your life.

Hold your crystal in your left hand and call to your spirit helper to focus the energy of the violet light through the crystal and permit the power to connect your consciousness to your higher self. Feel the violet light moving over you in a wave of warmth. See it touching every part of your body. Feel it interacting with every cell.

Now say inwardly or outwardly to your totem guide: "Beloved guide, assist me in calling upon the highest of energies from the Great Mystery. Activate my highest self to channel directly to the Oneness. Permit the violet light to move around and through me. Allow the transmutating energy of the Great Mystery to elevate all impure desires, incorrect concepts, all anger, all wrongdoing, all fears. Keep the light of the Great Mystery bright within me. Replace all negative, chaotic, fearful vibrations around me and in me with the pure energy, the power of accomplishment, and the fulfillment, of the Great Mystery."

### An Everyday Affirmation to Eliminate Fear and Negativity

You may also state this affirmation each morning upon arising: "Beloved Spirit Helper, I feel your energy on this new day activating my higher self and charging me with perfect health, joy, love, and the elimination of all fears and negativity."

### When Discord or Evil Is Directed at You

If you should feel discord or evil directed toward you in a crowded place, do the following:

1. Remove your crystal from your spirit bag and place it in your left hand.

2. Cross your arms over your solar plexus.

3. Put your knees or your feet together. If you are sitting, cross your legs. (The above actions instantly symbolize that you are not receptive, open, to discord.)

If you are in a social situation and feel that someone present is seeking to bombard you with negativity, do the following:

1. Hold your crystal in your left hand.

2. Move your arms across your solar plexus.

3. Cross your knees if seated.

4. Visualize your spirit helper in the midst of a circle of blue flames that moves down from the Great Mystery and positions itself between you and the person or the condition that is afflicting you with negative vibrations.

Such immediate action can block the vicious energy that is being directed at you. In addition, take fairly short breaths for a time—inhaling shallowly, but exhaling in a somewhat forceful manner.

This procedure should not be practiced overlong, but with enough time to express your resolve that you are not even breathing in the negativity that has been transmitted in your direction.

### WHEN EVIL STRIKES IN A STRANGE ENVIRONMENT

Suppose that you are in a strange environment and you have just been bombarded with negativity from a vicious person or by a situation that has left you feeling rather defeated and demoralized—and very much alone in the world. Try the following exercise:

Go to a place where you can be alone to re-establish your emotional and spiritual equilibrium. Sit quietly for a moment.

After you have begun to calm yourself, take your crystal from your spirit bag and hold it in your left hand. As you inhale a comfortably deep breath, say, "I am . . . As you exhale slowly, say, ". . . relaxed." Repeat this procedure a number of times. Take comfortably deep breaths. "I am . . ." asserts the sovereignty of your individual being on the intake. "Relaxed" positively affirms your calm condition on the exhalation.

Now gaze into your crystal and visualize the image of your spirit helper looking back at your. Feel the strength, the power, and the love of your totem animal.

Look into the crystal again and visualize your animal totem with someone who is extremely positive and who shares your point of view about life, who embraces your philosophy, your spiritual path, your perspective of reality. This may be a spouse, a lover, a friend, a family member, a mentor.

See the person on whom you are now focusing smile at you. See the person extending his or her hand to yours. Feel the touch of fingertip to fingertip. Sense the electrical crackle of energy moving between you. Experience the warmth of the love that flows between you.

Know and understand that the shared love between you and your spirit helper, between you and this person who loves you, has the power and the ability to erect a barrier between you and the negative bombardment to which you have just been subjected. Hold the images of your loving and harmonious totem animal and your human companion as long as you need them.

When you have become completely fortified and calmed, it would be best to go to bed and enjoy a peaceful and regenerative sleep.

If such a tranquil retreat is impossible and you must return to the encounter, know that you will do so totally reinforced and strengthened for any additional negativity that might be directed at you. Stride confidently back into the arena, knowing that you are linked together on the spirit level with your animal totem and a kindred soul who shares your perspective and your spiritual path.

# CHAPTER 9

# The Healing Powers of Totems

Sʜᴀʀᴏɴ Rᴀᴍᴍᴏɴ, ᴀ Wɪsᴄᴏɴsɪɴ resident of Irish-Cheyenne heritage, told me of a soul healing that Wolf, her totem animal, had accomplished for her during a severe emotional trauma. Although the experience was highly personal, I asked Dream Walker (Sharon's spirit name) to tell me as much about her interaction with Wolf as she felt could be shared with others.

Sharon began by saying that the extreme emotional pain of this trauma was such that it created a void in her life. "I was left in darkness without strength, love, or the will to exist. I was beyond even caring about what might happen to me."

During this terrible time, she began having dreams—extraordinarily vivid dreams—so powerful that she truly felt as though she were in a physical place. "At first I was in the forest, walking through a totally moonless night. Even though I felt as if I were being watched, I had no fear—because I had a single goal in mind. At the edge of the forest I knew that there was a bluff—and a very long drop to the rocks below. My intention was to walk off the bluff. To my way of thinking at that time, my only solution to my emotional pain was to end my life."

Each night as Sharon walked the forest in her dreams, she drew closer and closer to the bluff before she would awaken. And each night she could sense something following her.

"At first I saw just the eyes, but slowly my spirit guide came out of the shadows. It was my Wolf. We exchanged glances, but it took a few nights before we crouched beside one another, only a breath apart, looking deep into each other's eyes. Although he willingly shared his knowledge with me, I still could not rise above the pain that had seared my spirit.

"And then my goal had been reached. The edge of the bluff was near. I walked that last night alone. My guide was nowhere in sight."

Deeply saddened, Sharon truly felt that she had now lost everything, her new spirit friend included. She stood at the edge, her foot inching closer to the void.

"And then he was there, sitting at my side, watching me. I felt a tear fall from my eyes. Wolf took my hand in his mouth and began pulling me back, farther and farther from the edge.

"We sat together for a very long time, just sharing, communicating without words. I knew within his understanding and his love. Mentally, he showed me all the things that his kind had gone through for centuries, and the first great lesson that he taught me was to never give up. There is always another sun, another moon, another chance to make things right. There is always hope."

Since that time a few years ago, Sharon Rammon continues to be taught, guided, and soothed in her dreams or in a dream state. She has learned that her guide's name is Running Water, and they still share many walks in the forest—but now the moon is bright and the waterfall sings in the distance.

"I have always been attracted to wolves. When my wolf and I communicated for the first time, the lesson that he taught me was to never give up, that there is always a positive solution to every problem. I saw him through flashes of long ago when wolves were able to survive in their natural way."

Sharon said that she finds it very comforting to have a lot of pictures, statues, and other depictions of wolves, around the house.

"This past summer, my husband bought me a plate as a surprise. And there was my wolf. I almost dropped the plate when I opened the gift and saw him—a blue-black wolf with silver highlights. My husband knows nothing of my dreams and my spirit guide. Such things are not for him. So the plate he bought me has a special place of honor, and I keep a candle burning by it when I am home. It is a beacon of welcome to Running Water in spirit—because his heart and mine are one."

In her account of her interaction with her spirit helper, Sharon said that guidance and teaching come to her in different ways:

When my days are hectic and trying, I merely cry out, "Help! This is too much for me. I don't want to feel this anger or whatever." I ask to feel the calmness that I experience when my guide is near. Then, in spirit, I travel with Wolf to a place that is quiet and uplifting. I can hear a waterfall and birds singing.

How this is done is not easy to explain to some people, but it works for me. Running Water has shown me how to listen to my inner self and to improve my self-esteem and my outlook on life. All I can say to people is that I know that their own totem animal is waiting in spirit to guide and assist them.

Wolf does not dictate to me what I must do. But his wisdom is ancient, and when I come to a crossroads in life, all I have to do is ask for his advice and the answer is there inside my head—and I am surrounded by so much love that I want to burst. It feels so good to be accepted for myself. To be loved for who I am. Not for who I could be, but for who I am.

Wolf is also my protector, and knowing this is an awesome feeling. He is so strong, and he enfolds me in a warm blanket of security.

I am aware that there are higher planes of consciousness to reach, and he is taking me there. A couple of nights ago, I was taken on a trip. I don't know exactly where, because not all is revealed at once.

When I awoke the next morning, I felt so relaxed and happy, but I had a little doubt that maybe I had imagined the spirit journey. Then all around me I heard the most beautiful tribal music, with drums and all. That was my confirmation that the experience had been real.

At times my dog will suddenly look at a spot and start barking. It's always the same spot. I get chills and goosebumps, and I know that Wolf has come.

Wolf has taught me that life is special. Everyone has a job or a duty to complete. Big or small, the importance is no greater. Each link in the chain of life contributes to the smoothness of the cycle. To break any link in a untimely manner prevents the chain of events to be fulfilled as required.

My kinship with my totem animal is growing, and since you asked me to share a teaching from Running Water with others, I will say this: "My friends, you are the one in control of your life. You create it and direct it—and if you learn to do so with harmony and discipline, you will come to know the true spirit of freedom."

## AN OLD FOLKTALE'S LESSON

In order to fully understand that all creatures are relations, from the very largest to the very smallest, tribal youngsters were told such tales of animal caring and concern for humans as the following folktale of the Awana tribe of California:

Two little boys had been playing in the Yosemite Valley, swimming, paddling, splashing about to their hearts' content. When they lay down on a boulder in the warm sunshine, they fell into a deep sleep. So deep, in fact, that they slept through many moons, through winter snows and summer sun.

Meantime, the great rock on which they slumbered was rising treacherously higher day and night, until it had soon lifted them higher than any human could see, far beyond the sight of the family and friends who continued to search for them. The rock rose so high that it surely seemed as though the boys' faces would soon touch the moon.

The compassionate animals were touched by the tears of the mothers and fathers and the brothers and sisters who searched for the two boys; and because of their superior senses, they soon determined that the lost boys lay fast asleep on the great, towering rock. Now the problem of how they would rescue the boys and bring them back down to earth presented itself.

Each animal decided to make a leap up the face of the wall as far as he could spring and see if he could reach the top. Mouse could only jump up a handbreadth. Rat, two handbreadths. Raccoon, a little bit higher.

Bear stood waiting his turn, allowing the smaller animals to make a sincere effort at scaling the tower. His great leap carried him far up the rock, but he fell back like all the others before him.

The powerful, majestic Cougar was the last of the animals to heed the humans' cry for help. He flexed his magnificent muscles, stretched taut his mighty sinews, and made a leap that took him nearly to the clouds. But, alas, he, too, fell down flat on his back.

Then came along the tiny, insignificant Measuring Worm, with a body so soft and vulnerable that Mouse could have crushed it by treading on it accidentally. To the amazement of all those assembled at the foot of the great rock, Worm began to creep up the formidable tower.

Inch by inch, a little at a time, he measured his way up. It didn't take him long to match Mouse's leap or Rat's or Raccoon's. And then he had passed Bear's mighty jump and even Cougar's majestic leap.

He crawled up and up, through many sleeps and one whole snow, but at last he reached the top. Then he awakened the little boys and brought them safely to the ground.

And to this day, the rock is called Tutokanula, the Measuring Worm.

## Calling Upon Animal Totems for Healing

Once again we are going to pay a visit to our quintessential Shaman, the one we met in Chapter 3 when we were seeking greater awareness of our spirit helpers. Since we are now quite familiar with the Shaman's excellent credentials, we will come right to the point of our return visit: We are in need of healing. If you wish, of course, you may visualize a friend or a loved one in your place.

If you read the following visit to a Shaman aloud, it can truly become a very effective self-healing mechanism. Or you may wish to read it to a friend or loved one who is in need of healing. As a literary device, the visit is structured as you, the reader, and I, the author, travel together to ask the Shaman for healing. You may substitute at any time the pronouns "we" and "our" and so forth, for the names of your friend or family member.

As we did during our first encounter with the Shaman, we have brought an offering of tobacco or sweet grass to be given to the spirit beings through the agency of fire. And as before, you may visualize the Shaman in either male or female human form.

The elder opens the flap of the darkened Medicine lodge and we are ushered forward to be purified with the smoke of the burning sage. Then, once again, we sit before the fire and the Shaman on his mattress of buffalo hides.

The Shaman speaks:

As I offer tobacco to the spirit guardians, you must listen carefully. If you feel that I speak truthfully, you will gain strength. If you feel that I speak truthfully with the spirits of the animal guardians, I know that you will be healed. To remain healthy, you must help yourself as much as you can to live a strong and centered life and to walk in balance on the Earth Mother.

Ho! First I offer tobacco to the spirits of the Grandmothers and Grandfathers who live in the fire. Listen, O Ancient Ones, to the plea of those who are now as you once were. There are human beings before you who wish to be healed, who wish to live.

O grandparents, I ask that you remove the infirmity of these humans before you. I ask that the humans before you be restored to good health within no more than three days.

*O humans who wish to be healed, receive the spirit energy of the Ancient Ones into your body, mind, and spirit. May you continue to open to their healing power.*

Ho! O Buffalo Spirit, add your strength and power to the energy of these infirm humans who come before you seeking healing. When I lived in your lodge, first as a spirit, then as a buffalo, you blessed me with the healing power of the pure White Buffalo Spirit. You promised to come when I would summon you to breathe your strength into those who are ill. This is what I now desire. Here is your tobacco. Breathe health upon the ones who sit before you.

*O humans who wish to be healed, receive the curative power of the breath of the great Buffalo Spirit into your body, mind, and spirit. May you continue to open to its healing power.*

Ho! O Bear Spirit, here is tobacco for you brought by humans who wish to be healed. None have the great magic and power that you possess. When I lived among you as one of your kind, I studied your medicine and fasted on a long vision quest. You promised that you would send blessings on whomever I asked. I ask now for your blessing upon these infirm human beings before you.

*O humans who wish to be healed, receive the medicine blessing of the breath of the great Bear Spirit into your body, mind, and spirit. May you continue to open to its healing power.*

Ho! O Fish Spirit, here is tobacco offered to you. When I lived among you in the river, you promised me that I would have the blessing of the water energy to cleanse the body and to wash away sickness and all infirmities. Here now are human beings before you who wish to be healed and to live. I, too, wish that they be healed and live. I now take water from this bowl before me and sprinkle it over the bodies of the infirm ones seated before me. Grant these humans your curative powers.

*O humans who wish to be healed, receive the cleansing power of the water and take into your body, mind, and spirit the healing energy of the breath of the Fish Spirit. May you continue to open to these two great healing powers.*

Ho! O Spirit of the Raven, humans who wish to be healed have brought you an offering of tobacco. You have the power to fly high aloft with illness and infirmity and to send it to the Sun to be consumed by sacred flames. Your spirit can free the humans' spirits from their fleshly bonds and elevate them to restored health. Remember your promise to me to bless those whom I bless. Grant these humans your healing gifts.

*O humans who wish to be healed, receive the curative energy from the wings of the Raven Spirit into your body, mind, and spirit. May you continue to open to its healing power.*

Ho! O Rattlesnake Spirit, when my spirit entered into a body like yours and crawled beside you, you blessed me after I had fasted and studied your ways of ancient wisdom. You promised me then that you would always send healing power in your rattles and that whomever I blessed with my rattle, you also would bless and heal. Here is an offering of tobacco for you. I am asking now that you fulfill your promise and heal these humans before you.

*O humans who desire healing, hear the sound of my rattle, feel the curative powers of the breath of the Rattlesnake Spirit enter your body, mind, and spirit. May you continue to open to its healing energy.*

Ho! O Turtle Spirit, you who brings peace to all who heed your wisdom. When I lived among you as one in harmony and studied your teachings of peace, you promised me when you blessed me that I, too, would be able to restore balance to the physical body. You promised me that I would be able to extract pain and suffering, no matter how terrible it might be.

Here now are humans who have pain. I know that I am the one to remove their suffering, for you swore to me that I would not fail when I sought to restore harmony to the body. Here is your tobacco. I am going to heal these humans!

*O humans who wish to be healed, receive at once within your body, mind, and spirit the restoration of peace and harmony from the breath of the great Turtle Spirit. May you continue to open to its healing energy.*

Ho! O Spirit Beings, you promised that the sound of my flute was blessed with the power to heal. These humans have brought an offering of tobacco for you. Remember your promise, for I am going to heal these humans seated before you.

*O humans who wish to be healed, feel within your being the healing vibration of my flute. Feel the healing power of my breath upon your faces. May you continue to open to this curative energy.*

Ho! Disease-Giver! I feel your presence here. When I was a spirit in the world above, I watched you prowling about down on the Earth Mother. I saw you bringing sickness and illness to humans. You may believe that you have great power, but my totem helpers and the Grandparents in our original home have blessed me with the ability to heal.

Disease-Giver, you know that I have the promise of all my spirit helpers and all good spirits to stand by me when I desire to heal. Here is tobacco for you. You must accept the offering and leave these humans at once!

O humans who wish to be healed, reject the grip of Disease-Giver upon your body, mind, and spirit. Tell Disease-Giver that it is time to go . . . now! See Disease-Giver leaving you . . . now!

Ho! Great Mystery, mighty chief of all spirits, you have generously given us your gift of life. You have blessed me often, and you have promised always to help me help others. I offer you tobacco and ask you also to send healing to these humans and grant that they may live long on the Earth Mother. Ho-o-o. May it be so!

### TECHNIQUES OF HUNA HEALING PRAYERS

Some Huna practitioners seek to project *mana* through the hands of the members of a healing circle and to use their combined wills to make the *mana* flow into someone upon whom their hands had been laid.

In addition, they might then recite a prayer for healing, such as the following:

Father-Mother [Great Mystery], we hold this friend of ours to the Light for healing. Give him/her life.

Max Freedom Long advised that in such healing circles it is best to select a leader. All members might participate in the composition of a special healing prayer, but Max felt that it should be recited only by the leader, the "priest" of the circle, while all other members remained with their hands on the subject in a quiet and prayerful attitude. The prayerful quiet should be held for at least half a minute, then the leader of the circle should end the group prayer with words similar to the Kahunas of old:

Our prayer takes flight. Let the rain of blessings fall. *Ah-mana-mana!*

The idea, Max said, is to close the prayer action and not let it hang dangling: "Regular practice often will develop increasing healing ability. Frequently, if there are regular healing sessions being held, the disembodied spirits of people who were healers in life will be attracted to the sessions so that they might help direct the *mana* into the ones who are seeking healing."

As we have previously stated, *mana* goes where it is directed and does what it is asked to do—if one has full confidence, the low-self believes that what is being done will get results.

"A doubting Thomas or two in a healing group is bad," Max warned. "If people cannot be reasonably positive and expect results, then it is better that they draw out of the group and permit the rest of the circle to do the healing work."

*Mana* will travel or be projected, not only direct physical contact—which is easiest—but along the line of sight to a person.

The help that you can give yourself with auto-suggestion is also great, but like other ways of projecting or manipulating the *manas* of the body, you must slowly train the low-self and get it to understand what part it is to play in the healing work.

"A few people can use the art almost at once," Max said. "The majority will need practice over a period of a week or more before results become apparent. Some may never master the method for themselves, but they may be helping by having another person sit with them and give them suggestions."

## DRAW UPON YOUR TOTEM ANIMAL'S STRENGTH FOR REJUVENATION

When you are feeling at a low energy level because of an illness and you must have instant strength, visualize your spirit helper, say, for example, the Wolf. Then petition the Great Mystery in this manner:

> O Great Mystery, I am in need of strength.
>
> Charge me with the strength of my spirit helper, Wolf. [*Say the name of your own guide*] Charge me with his light and his love. Charge each of my vital body functions with the strength, energy, and power of my totem animal. And keep me ever attuned to your guidance and your direction.

## CREATING HEALTH THROUGH YOUR TOTEM AND CRYSTAL POWER

It is a tradition among certain Native American healers that a crystal to be used for healing should be given to you. I have had a number of crystals presented to me by powerful healers over the past thirty years and I have been privileged to have employed them in some dramatic healings channeled from the Great Mystery and my totem animals. Even as I write this, my special crystal rests just above my left shoulder encircled by a photograph of my wife, Sherry, and small statues of an angel, four owls, two frogs, and a winged cougar. (My eagle/bear/wolf totem is behind me, and three pictures of wolves guard the front room.)

This is not to say, of course, that you cannot go out and purchase a crystal on your own and invest your spiritual energy within it. If you apply your inner resources with sincerity, you may achieve a miraculous change in your health pattern.

For this exercise it is necessary for you to be able to sit quietly in a place where you will be undisturbed by all external stimuli for at least thirty minutes. Calm yourself and attempt to clear your mind of all troublesome thoughts.

For maximum results, I would recommend that you first read the technique to familiarize yourself with its concepts, then record yourself reading the exercise so that you may play it back and allow your own voice to guide you through the procedure. As an additional aid to the process, you might play some inspirational or soothing background music to heighten the effect. Be certain, though, that the music contains no lyrics to distract you and that you are meditating at a time and in a place where you will not be disturbed for at least thirty minutes. Your success in this exercise depends upon your willingness to permit a transformation to manifest in your consciousness, thereby allowing a dramatic healing process to occur in your physical body.

Take a moment to visualize the finest physical attributes of your totem animal—the powerful muscles, sinews, talons, or claws; its great powers of endurance; its keen eyesight or sense of smell or hearing, and so forth. Then see your totem animal resting at ease at your side, ever ready to respond to your wishes.

Take your crystal in your left hand. Holding the crystal thusly will stimulate the creative-intuitive process in the right brain hemisphere. The vortex of energy in the crystal will now begin interacting with your own electromagnetic field and will start to increase the field energy around you.

Now begin to breathe into your crystal your *intention* to bring the health, stamina, and strength of your totem animal into your body. Remember that one of the functions of the crystal is to magnify your intention.

Take a comfortably deep breath, hold it for the count of three, then exhale slowly.

Take another comfortably deep breath, hold it for the count of four, and exhale slowly.

And then a third comfortably deep breath, hold it for the count of five, and exhale very slowly.

Be aware that your Higher Self contains a magnificent blueprint of your perfect self, free from all sickness and pain. Form a mental image of yourself as you know you have the potential to become—an entity free from sickness and pain.

Place your crystal on the "third eye" area in the center of your forehead and hold the image of your Higher Self. This mental picture must make no reference to the pain or illness that you now suffer. You must only focus on your perfect self as you wish yourself to be.

Once you have fashioned that image of your perfect physical self, hold it fast and begin to breathe in very slowly, taking comfortably deep breaths. As you inhale, you are drawing in the *mana*, the *prana*, the *wakan*. Make and memorize the picture of your perfect self as you breathe and draw in the *mana*. It is the *mana* that will give the picture enough strength to hold together while the High Self begins to materialize the image into physical actuality.

Hold the picture in your mind as you continue to breathe slowly and to send energy to the Higher Self. *Live* in the picture. *Feel* it. Keep your mind from all negative thoughts to the contrary.

Permit yourself now to become totally relaxed. Lie back in a comfortable position and release all worries . . . all tensions . . . all problems. Imagine that you are lying comfortably and safely on the beach . . . in your back yard . . . in a peaceful meadow . . . wherever you wish. Imagine yourself in your ideal place to relax. Take three comfortably deep breaths and relax . . . relax.

Imagine before you now the softest, fluffiest cloud in all the sky settling down next to you as you relax . . . relax. See yourself crawling upon it to relax . . . to float . . . to relax . . . to rise to the sky and leave all your pain and illness behind you. You have no fear, for you know that your spirit helper is watching over you. The Great Mystery is watching over you. Leave your pain and your sickness down below you on the ground.

Float and drift, float and drift, rising into the sky in a comfortable, slow, swinging motion. Nothing will disturb you. Nothing will distress you. No sound will bother you. In fact, should you hear any sound at all, that sound will only help you to relax . . . relax.

Take three more comfortably deep breaths and relax . . . relax . . . as you drift and float higher and higher.

You are floating up into the sky, floating, drifting, relaxing. You feel safe and totally secure. It is impossible for you to fall. You know that your spirit helper is watching over you. You know that the Great Mystery is watching over you. You feel peace, love, and contentment.

All of your body is completely relaxed. Your toes . . . feet . . . legs . . . torso . . . arms . . . shoulders . . . neck . . . all are totally relaxed. Your entire body is completely relaxed . . . relaxed. All stress and tension have left your body. You have left all sickness and pain behind.

Now you are aware of a great bolt of energy that is shooting toward you. You know that it will not harm you in any way. It will, in fact, energize you. It is a bolt of energy that comes to you from your animal totem, your spirit helper, and it will give you strength and power.

Feel the soothing, yet exhilarating, warmth as this bolt of power from your animal totem touches your body. Feel the warm, tingling energy moving throughout your entire body. Feel the energy removing all pain, banishing all sickness.

You are now aware of another great bolt of energy moving toward you. It is another Lightning Bolt of Strength and Power directed at you from your spirit helper. You feel its warm energy touching you, giving you strength and power, driving away all pain, removing all sickness.

And now a third Lightning Bolt of Strength and Power touches and activates you with incredible energy. You feel a marvelous cleansing as the healing power of your animal totem moves throughout your entire body, giving you strength and power, banishing all pain, driving away all sickness.

You know that you will now be stronger than you have ever been. You will give full expression to the healing Lightning Bolts of Strength and Power from your spirit helper. Your very physical essence is glowing with the gift of healing.

Each and every cell of your body will obey the new energy of wellness and perfect health. Each and every cell of your body will heed the power and strength of your animal totem, which has now blended with you and removed all sickness and pain.

At the count of three, you will emerge from this state of relaxation eager to begin life anew with perfect health, with sickness and pain banished from your body. *One* . . . coming awake with renewed strength and wonderful health from your spirit helper. *Two* . . . coming awake with each cell, each sinew, each muscle, each organ renewed from the strength of your animal totem. *Three* . . . charged with the Lightning Bolt of Strength and Power . . . feeling better than you've felt in months and months . . . in perfect health as never before! Awaken!

# CHAPTER 10

# Receiving Initiation into Higher Awareness

**T**HERE ARE MANY WAYS OF RECEIVING initiation into higher levels of awareness, and there are many pathways leading to the mystic portal wherein lie the living visions that can grant you wisdom, knowledge, and illumination. At each level of consciousness, be cognizant that your totem animal waits to guide and protect you through the multiple mazes that comprise the testing grounds of planet Earth.

One of my greatest initiations into higher awareness occurred when I became one with all of nature through the psyche of a dying rabbit.

**139**

It was a beautiful day in early spring. I was sixteen, glorying in a wonderful day and the excitement of being alive. The last vestiges of snow and ice had melted into the fields, and farmwork would soon begin for Iowa country boys. But on this day, I was celebrating the promise of new life by plinking at tin cans with my slide-action Winchester .22.

And then I spotted him. At first I thought it must be a stray dog running across a plowed field. It was the largest jackrabbit that I had ever seen. This guy had to be the King of the Rabbits. And he was headed for the stand of trees in which I was target shooting. He was coming straight for me.

The Winchester in my hands seemed to vibrate with an energy of its own. *Shoot him! Shoot the rabbit!* It seemed as if the rifle were speaking to me. It was bored with lifeless tin cans. It wanted blood. It wanted a life.

I don't know why I could not be content to admire the huge rabbit's strength and beauty. Maybe he really was the King of the Jackrabbits. I don't know why I couldn't have been satisfied to appreciate him as another of the Creator Spirit's magnificent creatures.

To my shame, all I could think of was pulling the trigger. After all, what was the life of a big old rabbit, anyway? The .22 slug hit home, slamming the big rabbit off his graceful, loping stride and rolling him hard into a clump of grass.

As if I were a Great White Hunter in some African adventure film, I worked the slide and moved another cartridge into the breech. As if I were approaching a downed lion, I wanted to be ready with another shot to finish the deed if the beast should still be alive.

I was only a few feet from the rabbit when he arched up on his forepaws, looked directly at my face and made eye contact. I hesitated, uncertain of my next move, strangely intimidated by the rabbit's unwavering gaze.

And then with his last breath, he emitted a shrill, piercing death cry, "*Why?*"

I don't know how that scream might have sounded to you if you had been with me, but I heard that cry as an accusatory question that I knew I could not possibly answer.

*Why?*

I had no respectable or respectful answer. I didn't need his flesh for my food. I didn't need his fur for my clothing. He certainly posed no threat to me. I knew to my shame that I had only killed him for the sake of killing something that I considered lower than me on nature's totem pole.

And then a most remarkable occurrence took place. As I stood before the dying rabbit, feeling ashamed and unclean, there was a brilliant flash of light and suddenly I was seeing myself through his eyes. A skinny man-child in denim jacket, Levis, and boots, holding a deadly weapon in his hands.

But rather than feeling contempt or hatred for me for having taken his precious life so irresponsibly, he felt sad for me. He knew the secret. He knew that I had just killed a part of myself.

Somehow, in a way that my adolescent brain was only beginning to perceive through a darkened glass, the rabbit and I were linked together in some larger, truer vision of reality. Somehow, the rabbit and I were one.

And then there was another flash of that brilliant light, and I felt as if I were about to faint. My mind began to spin and reel.

In another flash of light, I suddenly felt as if I were one with the grass, with the pine tree, with a cloud moving overhead, with a crow sitting on a fence post. Then I *knew* that I was a part of everything and everything was a part of me. Somehow, wonderfully, beautifully, we were all One.

I fell to my knees before the rabbit and began to weep. I cradled his head in my hands and begged his forgiveness for my stupid, savage, selfish act.

The big rabbit shuddered and a bright red bubble of blood formed around his nostrils. He lay still and the bubble burst. He was dead. He could not grant me the forgiveness that I begged for to soothe my conscience.

And then, at last, I understood that only I could expiate my sin of senseless, selfish slaughter. It was up to me to remain in balance with the Oneness, with the Great Mystery, and to forever respect the individual sovereignty of all lifeforms on the Earth Mother. I never again wanted to gain illumination through the blood of another living thing. It was now up to me to make my own sacrifices, not to place the life of another of the Great Mystery's creations on the altar of my own shortcomings.

## To the Spirit World to See the Future

Laura Day is a forty-eight-year-old receptionist/office manager from Peru, Illinois, who has no difficulty blending her Episcopalian Christianity with the inspirational messages that she receives from her principal spirit teacher—who often takes the form of a hawk—or other tutelary animal totems. Of English, Cherokee, and Italian heritage, Laura was forty-two when she heard someone calling her name as she lay sleeping.

"The voice was very loud, and it awakened me," she said. "It called my name three or four times, but I could see no one."

It was not long after this activating incident that Laura's spirit teacher manifested and guided her to the other realm, which appeared to her as a beautiful canyon. It was in this sacred realm of visions that Laura learned to view Mother Earth as a spirit and was warned of events that are soon to transpire in a global process of cleansing and renewal.

In the following entries from her journal, Laura Day shares many of the warnings of future Earth changes and describes the symbology of her animal totems:

> *November 26, 1992:* It is not at the warm, beautiful canyon that I find myself, but in a place of pure white snow and high mountains. The sun is high and makes the snow sparkle. I do not feel the cold.
>
> My teacher, A-Shanti, appears and glides in on the air and begins to transform. Each time I see him change from hawk to human form, I am awed by the great power. I wonder which he would rather be, hawk or human.
>
> Knowing my thoughts, A-Shanti answers: "I am neither hawk nor human, but the spirits of both come together for one purpose—which is to enlighten my student in the other realm and to open your heart to that which is to come. I am a Native American spirit who has lived before on the land that I shall roam forever."
>
> A-Shanti then explains that we are in the frozen North, home of White One and old spirit friends. I ask who White One is.

"She is the most sacred blessing," A-Shanti replies. "She is from the Great Spirit and is the confirmation of His being. She is all goodness and love, but she has long been gone from the hearts of the people and has been forgotten."

My teacher instructs me to eat of the snow and to taste its sweetness. He says that we will be called to the North again when the snow is no more.

A-Shanti steps away from me. The light comes and transforms him to hawk. He glides toward the mountains and is gone.

*October 11, 1993:* A-Shanti appears and tells me he will be taking me to another sacred place, and he will show me what will happen in the near future. First, he says, I must close my eyes.

I close them and feel my teacher's hand on my shoulder. I can feel myself being lifted up. I become frightened, but in the next instant calm enfolds me. The force of the wind is so fierce that I feel tears forming in the corner of my eyes.

Then I feel myself being lowered, and I begin to regain my footing. A-Shanti says that I may now open my eyes.

We are on a mountain summit. When I look down into the valley below, I see a great spiral of hazy mist.

"Look and feel," A-Shanti says, "for what you are about to see will come soon. Hold all of this in your mind's eye and know within your spirit that it is so."

As my teacher stretches his right arm, the spiral mist below begins to swirl and ascend to the sky. What is revealed below is complete destruction. There is no plant life, and there are millions of dead and decaying creatures everywhere.

Although I don't see any humans below us, I ask A-Shanti: "Where are they?" He answers: "Many are as you see below. Only the ones with pure hearts who have love for Mother Earth and all of her creatures, who respect the Great Spirit, and who are one with the spirit will be left. The Red Wind has done all this—and it blows from the West."

[Note: After this vision I've prayed daily for the Great Spirit's blessing on Mother Earth and on all living things.]

*June 6, 1994:* [Note: The following vision has such great meaning for me because it was then that my teacher foretold the birth of the sacred White Buffalo. The White One comes!] The sacred canyon is beautiful and peaceful. My teacher appears before me and tells me: "A great sign will be given to the people of Earth. Some will know the meaning of this sign, others will not. It will come to Earth in the next couple of months. The Great Spirit's blessing and the renewal begins. The ways of the past are refreshed—for the White One comes!"

[Note: On August 20, 1994, a female white buffalo is born in Janesville, Wisconsin. When I heard of this, my heart rejoiced, for I know why she's been sent and why she returns to us.]

*August 14, 1994:* I am at the beautiful canyon, just as before. My teacher remains in his hawk form and glides with the thermals. He moves farther away from me and toward the opposite side of the canyon. Stretching out on the other side is a great plateau. He hovers above the plateau and gives his call four times.

A cloud begins forming above us, then descends, covering the plateau. The great cloud moves forward and stops at the very edge of the canyon wall.

A-Shanti glides toward me. A bright light enfolds him and his transformation takes place. As I watch, the light which had surrounded my teacher fades into nothingness.

When I return my eyes to the plateau, I perceive that the great cloud that was there has disappeared. What now stands before us on that plateau are a countless multitude of animals and a bridge of hazy mist that links the plateau to our side of the canyon. As I look at the incredible array of thousands upon thousands of creatures, I realize that there are some species that I have never before seen—and others which have been gone from Mother Earth for millions of years. And then I understand that what stands before us now are only the spirits of these creatures.

Among the great multitude of spirit animals, I do, of course, recognize the beings that are always with A-Shanti and me during my visions.

"Your friends have come to speak with you this day," says A-Shanti.

I respond that I am honored that they have come and I promise that I will listen to all they say with an open heart.

The first to cross the bridge of mist is Turtle. She carries upon her back a small golden frog. These are Turtle's words of warning: "My golden friend is in grave danger. Children of Mother Earth, heed the signs! When my golden friend is no more, our mother begins her change."

[Note: A news report in September 1994 stated that after studying a small golden frog in the South American jungle, baffled scientists announced the creature's complete disappearance.]

Turtle addresses me by my spirit name, and she gives thanks to the Creator Spirit for bringing all the animal spirits here this day. Then she says to me: "I am happy to know what is in your heart. I have known since the time of your birth that we would one day meet. It has taken until now for you to open your mind, heart, and spirit. You will now see as few others will. I will be with you often to guide you and to give you strength."

Turtle turns and slowly begins her journey back across the bridge.

Crow is the next to cross. He flies to A-Shanti's outstretched arm. He greets my teacher, then turns to face me. "You have grown in spirit and wisdom," he says. "Your path has been difficult, but it will soon be easier. I will guide you through darkness and light, for I am the link between the realms."

Crow plucks one of his tail feathers and drops it at my feet. He gives his thanks to the Great Spirit for bringing him here, and then he returns to the plateau.

Bear is next to walk across the misty pathway. A-Shanti greets him by laying his hand on his massive head. I can see the bond between these two powerful spirits and it gives me great joy.

Bear approaches me and says, "All life on Mother Earth has a spirit. We are the essence of the Great Spirit formed by His hand. He has created all things; therefore, all things are sacred and loved by Him. We are all brothers and sisters, even though we live our lives differently. You can learn from us. Remember, whether human, animal, winged ones, or fish in the waters, we are all one family and connected one to another. Call upon my spirit. I will hear and be with you. I will help you prepare for Earth's renewal."

Then Bear turns and lumbers back across the bridge.

From almost the very beginning of my visions, Wolf has been there. He is nearly always with my teacher and me.

Wolf is the last to come across the bridge. He greets my teacher, then lies down at my feet. Then, with his teeth, he picks up Crow's feather and offers it to me.

"We have met many times before," he says. "We know each other well. The future will give us much time together. I am your protector and your guardian. I will teach you and be with you each new sun and moon.

"The spirits are happy this day, for they are preparing for the birth of White One and the renewal of Mother Earth. When White One comes, she will be your confirmation of all that has transpired. I will be with you and at your side in both realms."

Wolf does not leave me to return across the bridge.

The cloud forms again, covering the multitude of creatures. Silver light fills the sky, then quickly disappears. When I look again, the animals which were on the plateau are gone as well.

A-Shanti's transformation is completed and he is Brother Hawk
once again. The canyon is as before—a sacred place in the other realm.

## Traveling in Spirit to a Sacred Place

You should be seated comfortably in a place and at a time when you
will not be disturbed for at least thirty minutes. Inspirational music
playing in the background could prove to be of great benefit in accel-
erating this exercise.

Your success will depend upon your desire to make contact with
your animal totem and to travel in spirit to a sacred place in a higher
realm. Be certain that you are in an extremely relaxed state before
the voice of a friend—or your own prerecorded voice—leads you
through the following process:

Summon some *mana* by taking three comfortably deep
breaths. Visualize the image of your totem animal just before
you take each breath.

Close your eyes and take a few moments to visualize your
concept of a sacred realm in another dimension of time, place,
and spirit. Visualize you and your spirit helper in this beautiful
spiritual realm.

As your body lies now in a very relaxed state, your mind, the
real you, is very much aware that you are being surrounded by
a beautiful golden light, and you feel the warmth of the light
from the Great Mystery beginning to stimulate your Crown
Chakra.

You are becoming one with the feeling of being loved unconditionally by your animal totem, your spirit helper. As you
begin to feel the presence of your totem guide, you are becoming aware of the sensation of warmth in both your Heart
Chakra and your Crown Chakra.

You are aware that your totem animal is approaching you in
a brilliant sphere of glowing light. See now that a ray of light is
connecting your Heart Chakra to the higher vibrations in the
sphere of glowing light.

The golden light begins to swirl around you until you see
that it takes the shape of your totem guide. Greet your spirit
helper. Tell it how much you love and appreciate it.

And now the purple mist of time and space is swirling around you and your spirit helper. The two of you are beginning to move higher toward another dimension of consciousness. You seem to be floating through space, moving gently through space, moving through all of time.

Time itself seems to be like a spiral moving around you, a spiral never ending, never beginning, never ending, never beginning.

Ahead of you, suspended in space, is a great golden portal. You know that with your spirit helper as your guide you will be able to move through that mystic portal and enter the dimension where visions live.

As your totem animal moves closer to you, as if to protect you, you move through the golden portal and step into the sacred place where visions live.

The first vision that approaches you is explaining to you your true mission in life. See clearly what it is that you are to accomplish in your earthwalk.

See clearly and understand what it is that you must do to better serve the Great Mystery as you accomplish your mission in life. See clearly and understand what it is that you must do to better serve the Earth Mother and all her creations as you accomplish your mission in life.

See clearly and understand how it is that your totem animal can better assist you in accomplishing your true mission in life.

Feel yourself being filled with a wonderful sense of well-being now that you know what you must do to fulfill your mission in life. You no longer feel sensations of frustration, guilt, or anxiety, as you see clearly how best to accomplish your mission in life.

As the first vision passes, you notice that your animal totem is opening its mouth. *Listen!* Listen to the sound that issues forth from your spirit helper's mouth. You hear it clearly and understand it. It may be a personal tone—a mantra, just for you. It may be a series of notes and words—your own personal song of attunement.

Whatever the sound is, you hear it clearly and distinctly. And you have the inner awareness that whenever you repeat this sound, this mantra, this song, you will be able to achieve instant at-oneness with your totem guide.

And now your spirit helper is showing you something very important. Your totem guide is showing you an object you can see clearly. This object is to serve as a symbol to you in your dreams. It will serve as a symbol that you are about to receive a meaningful and important teaching in your dream.

Whenever you see this symbol in your dreams, you will understand that whatever is to follow is an important and significant teaching intended just for you. The symbol fades from sight, but *you will remember it*.

And now your spirit helper is standing before a tiny flame, a flame such as one might see on a candle. The flame flickers and dances. You cannot take your eyes from it.

The flame seems to capture all of your attention and to pull you toward it. It is as if your very spirit is being pulled into the flame.

The flame is becoming brighter and brighter—brighter and larger. You cannot take your eyes from this strange and compelling flame. You can no longer see your totem animal. You can see only the flame. You are no longer aware of anything other than the flame.

The flame is growing larger and larger, brighter and brighter. It is as if there is nothing else in the entire universe other than the flame and you.

You know now that this flame is the Sacred Fire from the Great Mystery. You know that your spirit helper has brought this flame to you to bring you illumination. You know that it is not really a fire, not really a flame. You know that it is a holy and sacred energy, the same energy that is interwoven in all of life, the same divine energy that interacts with all living things.

The energy now swirls around you, lightly tingling the body whenever it touches you. It is not at all unpleasant. It is exhilarating and soothing at the same time. You are aware of your body being cleansed, purified, healed of any ills, pains, and tensions.

The energy of the Sacred Fire of the Great Mystery now enters your body. It is now becoming One with you.

In a great rush of color and light, you now find yourself elevated in spirit. You have moved to a dimension where nonlinear, cyclical time, flows around you. You are aware that you now exist in a Timeless Realm, an Eternal Now.

At this eternal second in the energy of the Eternal Now, at this vibrational level of Oneness with all living things, at this frequency of awareness of unity with the universe, the Great Mystery is permitting you to receive a great teaching vision of something about which you need to know for your spiritual growth. Receive this great vision now! (*Pause here for about one minute*)

You will awaken at the count of five, filled with memories of your great vision. When you awaken, you will feel a greater unity with your totem animal than ever before. When you awaken, you will feel the illumination of the Sacred Fire of the Great Mystery still inspiring you. When you awaken you will feel a renewed sense of Oneness with all living things.

*One* . . . coming awake, feeling better and healthier than ever before in your life. *Two* . . . more and more awake. *Three* . . . feeling a sense of Oneness with all living things. *Four* . . . coming awake with your spirit helper at your side. *Five* . . . wide awake and feeling wonderful!

When your spirit helper has given you a vision teaching in a spiritual exploration such as the one above, you will often find that a feeling of "knowing" has enveloped you. You suddenly "know" that you have always been aware of a particular cosmic truth that ostensibly you only just received.

When you tell others of the wisdom received in your teaching visions, you will soon discover that you are able to speak of truths beyond those which you consciously received at the time of the experience. This is because you have absorbed the higher dimensional frequencies that accompanied your spirit helper, and because you are being further elevated in spiritual consciousness by your act of telling others of your new insights. By giving, you receive in greater abundance.

All the teachings that will ever be relayed to you by your spirit helper are but parts of a single, living, vibrational truth that is composed of many facets. Depending upon your degree of personal awareness, you will at first comprehend the level of truth nearest your own understanding; but as you grow in wisdom, you will steadily perceive that all individual truths are connected one to the other, as if they were images on a great tapestry.

If you continue to work with your animal totem and to elevate your spiritual consciousness, you will one day be able to achieve the highest level of awareness and thereby envision the single great truth in its entirety. It is in this way that you will pierce the Great Mystery and become one with the Creator Spirit.

# Totem Animal Dictionary

THIS DICTIONARY OF ANIMAL TOTEMS is intended to be used by the reader as a tool in assisting in the attainment of a totem animal that may more clearly represent the spiritual goals of the initiate. The definitions are intended only to stimulate your personal evaluation and selection process. As indicated throughout the text, I urge you to follow the exercises and techniques provided in the various chapters and explore, study, and seek out the symbol of the spirit helper that is truly your very own.

Early in my journeys among the Medicine practitioners in search of spiritual wisdom, a Mohawk Shaman gave me some advice that I took very much to heart. "It is fine to be inspired by the ways and the teachings of others," he said, "but to get something truly good and powerful out of your visions, you should not be content to imitate or to copy what others already have received from the Great Mystery.

"You have the ability to receive your own Medicine in the same way that the native people have developed their power. Go to the waters and listen. Try to hear what the waters have to say. What is the essence of the spirit of the waters?

"The only formula is go into the Silence and sit and listen. This is what all sincere people should do, rather than trying to take over what has already been developed by native Shamans or other holy people. Your own true visions will teach you not to take on the identity of another, but to become your own real person."

I hereby pass on that sage advice to you. Go into the Silence and sit and listen. It really is the only formula that will enable you to receive your own true visions and enable you to become your own real person.

**Alligator/Crocodile**—To the ancient Egyptians the fearsome crocodile was often identified with Osiris, lord of the fertilizing power of the Nile, god of death and rebirth. The mighty water creature was also used as a symbol for reason, for it appeared to see clearly even though its eyes were covered by a protective membrane. The crocodile god, Sebek, was often associated with Ra, the creator Sun God.

To the Hebrews, the crocodile was leviathan, "the great dragon that lies in the midst of rivers" [Ezekiel 29:3] . . . "upon Earth there is not his like, who is made without fear" [Job 41:33]. Leviathan evolved from crocodile to a great demon dragon, synonymous to many as Satan.

Some African tribes believe that crocodiles house the souls of murder victims seeking revenge. A more common belief construct maintains that the great reptiles are themselves the present incarnations of tribal ancestors. And as powerful physical representations of Grandmothers and Grandfathers who have returned in spirit, they may be either benevolent guides or monsters to be feared.

The crocodile as a symbol of deceit grew from European travelers who claimed that they had witnessed the large reptiles luring their victims to the river's edge by moaning and crying as if in pain. Once the hapless investigator had been caught in its powerful jaws, it was alleged that the crocodile would continue to weep over its prey, crying "crocodile tears."

To the Native American tribes of the southeastern United States, the alligator certainly inspired reverence and respect, but it figures in the majority of folk stories as the butt of Rabbit's clever tricks. That audacious trickster was not always quick enough, however, for it was an alligator that snapped off Rabbit's once long and elegant tail, thus shortening it to its present ball of fluff.

Certain of those same tribes perceived evil spirits as bearing the same coarse scales of the alligator and maintained that the Master of Life had purposely created them with such rough and ugly skin to make their true natures readily identifiable to the discerning.

If you have recently acquired the alligator as your totem animal through a dream or a vision, you have an ally that will guide you to an understanding of deep levels of ancient wisdom that may be used for the acquisition of great personal empowerment. Your spirit helper will help you to sense wisely that such power brings with it the need for balance so that you do not abuse your strength.

The great reptile may also symbolize the figure of the proud survivor. The alligator has survived essentially unchanged for millions of years as a strong, tough, powerful, and fearless ruler of its domain. This spirit helper will always see to it that you acquit yourself proudly in any physical encounter on your earthwalk, but it will also see that you practice regular meditation so your spiritual growth is not neglected.

**Ant**—To the tribes of West Africa, ants are seen as messengers of the gods.

The Shamans of Morocco believe that to dream of ants is to envision the coming of prosperity.

In the cosmology of the Hopi tribe, the first humans were originally created as ants. Interestingly, the Nautoway tribe have a fable of an old man and woman who watched an anthill until they saw the insects change into white men and the seeds, which they carried in their mouths, into bales of merchandise.

The book of Proverbs advises the sluggard to go to the ant, "consider her ways and be wise." [6:6]

The ancient Greeks, who worshipped Ceres, goddess of fields and fruits, viewed ants as sacred, for they, too, industriously carried grains and seeds to their underground storage bins. And because they traveled freely both on and below the earth, ants were also used in the art of soothsaying. Their very movements were carefully considered as omens of guidance.

Moslems honored the ant as the earthly mentor of the great King Solomon, thereby acclaiming the insect as an embodiment of wisdom.

If you have chosen the ant as your totem animal or if the ant came to you in a dream or a vision quest, know that the ant may represent perseverance, industry, strength, and the very essence of the cooperative spirit.

The ant may have presented itself to you as a spirit helper because you have been too aloof from social concerns. Or you have felt powerless as an individual to make a difference. Although very small, the ant is disproportionately strong as an individual, yet chooses to work as a unit in a larger community.

The ant may sometimes symbolize a desire to achieve oneness and wholeness with the web of life on the Earth Mother, and your spirit ally will help you to understand clearly your important role in the plan of the Great Mystery.

**Antelope**—In the Mideast, the antelope was associated with the worship of the Great Mother. In India, the graceful animal belonged to Shiva, the destroyer.

While the antelope is found primarily in Africa, with a few species in Eurasia, wherever it exists its horns have been prized for their magical and medicinal properties. Certain African Shamans believe that an antelope horn is an excellent tool to keep a nasty spirit at bay.

An old Native American legend expresses a similar belief in the ability of deer horns to thwart evil. According to this story, the Great Mystery created Good and Evil as brothers. While the one went throughout the land making beautiful things, the other followed behind, destroying all of his brother's creations. When the two siblings eventually came to a violent confrontation, Good finally managed to subdue Evil by impaling him on deer horns.

In the United States, the pronghorn deer is often called an antelope. A number of Native American tribes believed that manitou energy frequently expressed itself in the antelope and that spirits of the deceased may temporarily assume its graceful, almost ethereal, form for a final walk on the Earth Mother before moving on to the place of the Grandparents.

As a totem animal, the antelope epitomizes grace, swiftness, and a nimbleness of spirit. Among the fastest animals in the world, the antelope may represent communication with higher levels of consciousness.

If you have chosen the antelope as your animal totem, you have an ally that will assist you in achieving great advancement in your spiritual evolution. At the same time, you will see great improvements reflected in your social and family life.

Ape/Gorilla—The great Chippewa Medicine Teacher Sun Bear once teased me by pointing out the great diversity of totem and clan animals available to traditional Native Americans.

"But the poor white folks seem to have only one totem animal, only one clan animal—the ape," he said, smiling broadly. "White people believe that they were all descended from the hairy ape. But it doesn't make any difference if some of us native people believe that we were descended from wolves, deer, or bears and you believe your ancestor was an ape. We should still all be able to get along in peace and harmony."

There were no apes or primates on the North American continent, but it is recorded that when the early missionaries showed the Delaware tribe pictorial representations of apes, the people concluded that the evil spirit had fashioned the creatures to mock the Great Mystery's creation of humans.

Many African tribes believe that the great apes are really capable of speech and that secretly, among themselves, they converse freely with one another. They refuse to do so in the presence of humans for fear that they might be put to work and made to live in villages with their hairless brothers and sisters.

A Jewish tradition maintains that God transformed some of the arrogant people who sought to stretch the Tower of Babel to Heaven's door into apes as punishment for their misdeed.

In Christian symbology, the ape represents unrestrained lust and the lowest and basest aspects of humankind's bestial nature. One tale even has Satan creating the ape as his corporeal counterpart to God's fashioning of the human. On the other hand, Hindu folklore often portrays the ape as a compassionate and helpful creature, such as the character of Hanuman in the Ramayana.

The ape, although tremendously powerful, is, unless provoked, a gentle animal. As a totem animal, the ape may represent self-control, self-discipline, and the confidence to express strength through gentleness and kindness. If you have chosen the ape as your spirit helper, be assured that you will begin to notice a new respect from your fellow workers and in your family environment.

While you are experiencing new physical accomplishments with the help of your totem guide, be certain that you do not neglect taking time to enter the Silence for your spiritual growth.

**Badger**—Although the badger is not a large animal, it is extremely strong, with powerful claws on its forefeet. Larger creatures many times its size will give the badger a wide berth.

The Zuni consider the badger the younger brother to the bear, respecting his strength and his stout heart, but criticizing him for what they assess as a much weaker will than that of his burly, big brother. The Zuni also envision the badger as the guardian of the South, quite likely due to the animal's ruddy coat, with its evenly marked black-and-white stripes, thus suggesting a being that stands between night and day, with the color of summer.

Other Native American tribes saw the badger's incredible prowess at burrowing through the earth as symbolic of the newborn child pushing its way through the womb. Mothers soon to deliver prized badger paw talismans as helpers to guide them through a brief period of labor.

Perhaps because of his supposed knowledge of the subsurface world, the Pueblo saw the badger as a great medicine chief, conversant with all manner of herbs, seeds, and the mysteries of plants.

The Japanese also respect the badger's strength, but most often cast him in a very negative role as a dangerous creature capable of violent acts. The badger is also perceived as a favorite form assumed by shape-shifting dark magicians.

The badger was on the Hebrews' list of unclean animals, but its skin was used for sandals.

As a totem guardian, the badger will be a strong protector and ally that will keep dark energies at bay. Because of its rather aggressive nature, however, you must be certain that you remain balanced in temperament and judgment so that violent responses to difficult situations are never encouraged.

**Bat**—Most tribal Shamans regard the bat as an evil omen. Perhaps the creature's very appearance suggests a kind of moral ambivalence, for it is difficult to ascertain if the swiftly flying nocturnal beastie is a bird with a rodent's snout and teeth or a rat with a bird's wings.

A number of the plain's tribes have a tale in which the handsome and mysterious bat successfully woos his wives by night—only to have them run away in the light when they see how ugly he is.

"If you have dreamt of a bat," a Medicine practitioner once told me, "you must be prepared for bad quarrels and much unpleasantness to come at you right around the next corner."

However, I have heard other Native Americans place a positive connotation on the bat, for they regard him as a rainmaker who drives away drought. And there are African tribes that esteem the bat as a sign of wisdom, for behold how unerringly it can maneuver through the darkness.

In Christian folklore, perhaps especially in Central Europe, the bat is considered the bird of Satan, a night-flying, blood-sucking entity that can actually become a vehicle for the Master of Hell. Such beliefs stay with us, firmly anchored in the popular fright night figure of Count Dracula spreading his dark cape to transform himself into a bat.

Batman, another pop culture figure, also embodies the mysterious ambiguity of his namesake. A flawed hero, with a great many deep-seated psychic scars, the face of the rich and handsome Bruce Wayne is covered in a frightening mask when he becomes the dark knight of vengeance.

To the Chinese, the bat represents happiness and longevity. If five bats should visit one's home, one has been blessed with the five blessings of health, wealth, long life, peace, and happiness. On the other hand, the Japanese seem to perceive in the bat's ambiguous nature a symbol of chaos and unhappy confusion.

Among certain of the Australian Aborigines and other Pacific peoples, the bat is synonymous with the human soul; and to find a dead bat is to be made aware that someone has made his transition to the other world.

If the bat appeals to you as a totem guardian, you may very well be a very adaptable person who has little fear of the Dark Side. You have probably been blessed with a keen sense of wonder and the willingness to explore with zeal topics which others may consider "forbidden" or "too far-out."

As a totem animal, the bat will be ever ready to guide you safely through the darkness of confusion and to lift you to higher realms of consciousness. Its built-in "radar" makes this totem guardian a skillful pilot through the darkest trials of the spirit. And it will always be a sure navigator as you enter the Silence and receive inspiration from the Great Mystery.

**Bear**—The bear is so highly revered as a totem animal that many Medicine priests have adopted "bear" as a part of their name. According to some tribes, the spirit of the bear never dies, and thus has become synonymous with supernatural powers and the ability to heal. Among nearly all shamans, the bear is reverently addressed as "Grandfather."

Throughout the globe and since the Neanderthal cave dwellers, humans who live in proximity to bears begin to make comparisons to themselves and their powerful woodland neighbor. The Native Americans were no exception, noting that just like the people of the villages, the bear is able to live on fish, flesh, or berries. The lumbering giant was known for its great love of honey, and its keen sense of smell was able to detect the golden sweet treasure of a bee hive from miles away. The tribespeople watched in awe as their powerful brother snatched the honey from the hive without fear of being stung.

When the bear was on the hunt, it seemed to saunter in a leisurely manner, its huge feet placed flat upon the ground and turned slightly inward, thereby causing the forest giant to walk with a peculiar movement. When it stood upright on its two hind feet, it appeared very much like a stout, powerfully built man with short, bandy legs. But the tribal hunters knew better than to confront a bear in such a position, for from such a stance it would attack its enemies, using the claws in its great forepaws to slash at the head and the belly with devastating results.

The Navajo regard the bear with as much respect as any of their human neighbors. They kill bears only when necessary, and under no conditions would a Navajo eat a single bite of bear meat. In their eyes, it would be like chewing on the spirit of their ancestors.

Among the old tribes of Northern Europe, the Nordic warriors, known as the "Berserkers," wore bearskin shirts into battle in dedication to the Goddess Ursel, the She-Bear. To the Norse, the bear was a masterful martial artist, and the she-bear protecting its cubs was the worst nightmare a hunter could encounter under the Northern lights. Thus, the bearskin shirts were worn in the hope that the warrior could absorb the great beast's fighting prowess and its enormous endurance and strength. To the Viking warrior, the bear symbolized the lonely champion, prepared to fight in single combat.

The bear was a totemic symbol for St. Gall and St. Seraphim. In the Native American zodiac, those born from August 22 to September 22 are in the Medicine Wheel sign of the bear. Bear people are said to be slow, cautious, and quiet.

To have the bear as your totem animal is to be aware that you are being guided to assume a role of leadership. Your spiritual guardian will also encourage you to exercise your abilities as a natural healer.

You may also be placed in a position in which you will need to defend your beliefs in a firm and fearless manner, but your bear totem will give you the insight and powers of discrimination to present the truths of your lifepath with confidence and courage. Follow your bear as your totem guide, and you will be led to greater balance in body, mind, and spirit.

**Beaver**—The Osage tribe has a charming legend about how the first human evolved from a snail, Wabashas, who upon receiving the blessing of the Great Spirit was presented with the gift of a bow and arrows. While Wabashas strutted along the riverbank, enjoying his new position as lord of his domain, he was suddenly confronted by a large beaver who identified himself as the Chief of the Beavers, lord of all the rivers and streams, and a very, very busy person.

Sensing conflict and truly wishing to avoid it, Wabashas informed Chief Beaver that the Great Spirit had recently placed him at the head of beasts and birds, fishes and fowls, and had given him the bow and arrows with which to maintain his position. Once Chief Beaver viewed the sharp points on the heads of the arrows, he modified his position and announced that he had perceived that humans and beavers should be brothers.

Wabashas accepted an invitation to his lodge in the river, and when the chief's wife and daughter brought in the choicest food known to them—fresh peeled poplar, willow, sassafras, and elder bark—he was immediately enamored of the charms of Chief Beaver's lovely daughter. Unable to take his eyes from her, he begged Chief Beaver to grant him his daughter's hand in marriage. Seeing that the maiden was also attracted to the handsome Wabashas, the Chief did not hesitate to grant his consent. A marriage quickly followed with a grand feast to which all friendly animals were invited.

Thus, from the union of the snail and the beaver, the Osage tribe had its origin. And all tribes, perhaps especially the people of the northeast, felt great affection for the beavers in their streams, referring to them as the Little Wise People.

While the white man made an industry of the fur trade, focusing at first on the beaver pelt to be fashioned into hats, the Native Americans revered the skin of the beaver to have medicinal powers. To many Shamans of the northeastern tribes, manitous, or spirit beings, also fancied the beavers as companions and bequeathed their healing abilities to the Little Wise People.

In the Medicine Wheel of the Native American zodiac, beaver people are those born from April 20 to May 20. They are generally healthy, loyal to their friends, and cherish peace and security.

If you are attracted to the beaver as your totem animal, you are probably a hard-working, no-nonsense kind of person. As a spirit guide, the beaver will bring you a sense of stability and renewed energy. You will probably find yourself becoming even more resourceful and practical than before. Just as the industrious beaver steadfastly chews down trees to shape a new and different environment in rivers and streams, so will the beaver as your totem animal encourage you to restructure the things in your personal environment that displease you.

As a small caution, do not permit your steadfastness to become just plain stubbornness. If you reinforce your spirit contact with adequate time in the Silence of meditation, your very own Little Wise Person will help you keep your balance.

Bee—The bee seems to be a universal symbol of diligence, obedience, and the work ethic. Many ancient cultures considered bees to be the messengers of the gods. The "busy" little bee in a number of traditions also becomes a symbol of the human soul. The bee is a totem symbol for St. Ambrose and St. John of Chrysostom.

The sign of the bee in Egyptian hieroglyphs seems to be analogous to royalty, epitomizing the ideals of industry, creativity, and wealth, which are associated with the diligent insects' production of honey. A very old myth portrays the bee as having been created from the tears of Ra. In Medieval Europe, the myth was converted to the bees having originated from the tears of Christ on the cross.

In ancient Greece, bees were considered to be the surviving souls of priestesses who in their physical lives had served the goddess Aphrodite. Mortal priestesses were called *melissae* (bees). According to tradition, the second of the great temples constructed at Delphi was constructed by bees.

In British folklore, bees are often associated with mortality. If bees are seen to be vacating a hive, it is an omen that the beekeeper is not long for this world. It was also customary to "tell" the bees when there was a death in the family so they would not fly away to another hive.

Among Native American tribes of the eastern seaboard, an old children's song laments the sad fact that the hardworking bee has only one stinger with which to defend the honey that all creatures—including humans—seem to prize so highly: The poor little bee/That lives in a tree/The poor little bee/That lives in a tree/Has only one arrow/In his quiver.

Grandmother Twylah of the Seneca has said that the bee is the symbol of an industrious, selfless, self-sufficient person who can deal with great success in a wide range of activities.

If the bee is your totem guide, you will be given help in organizing the chaos and confusion that life can often deal to us humans. You may also expect help in cultivating your social skills. Your spirit helper will serve you well as a messenger to the Great Mystery, and it will also bring you messages from higher realms of consciousness in your dreams and visions.

An entity of peaceful organization and construction, the bee will also teach you how to keep your "stinger" sheathed until you really need it.

**Boar**—Among the old Irish, the pig became a spiritual symbol, and it was believed that the boar and its sow had a firm association with the Other World and had absorbed much transcendental wisdom.

The honor of carving the boar at banquets and distributing portions of the meat went to the bravest among the village heroes. Celtic warriors placed an image of the vicious fighting boar on their shields, helmets, and swords.

The Welsh Triads pay tribute to Henwyn, a gigantic sow known as the Great White One, that brought forth to the people wheat, barley grain, and honey. Clearly a fertility symbol, Henwyn, also known as Cerridwen or Cerdo, was said to be the possessor of a marvelous magical cauldron and the mother of the great hero Taliesin.

In pre-Christian Spain, the Celto-Iberians erected large figures of boars beside their villages to encourage prosperity to visit them. Harvest dances were called *cerdana,* "pig dances," in honor of the sow goddess who gave new life, but who, in the fullness of time, harvested souls.

The old Vikings believed that the image of a boar on a warrior's helmet would serve as a protector in battle. They also fashioned great boar masks, complete with large, protruding tusks to frighten their opponents in combat. The legendary hero Beowulf possessed a boar's head helmet that no sword could penetrate.

Among the Germanic and Scandinavian tribes, the boar god came to represent both death and rebirth. Sacrificed at Yul with an apple in its mouth, "Valhalla's swine" was cooked in a cauldron and eaten ceremonially.

One of the most fitting tributes to the remarkable fighting prowess of the boar occurred when armies of warriors bequeathed its name to the wedge battle formation, which was called *cuneus* by the Roman legions and *caput porci* (boar's head) or *svinfylking* by the Scandinavian and Germanic tribes.

The Indian cult of Vishnu pays tribute to the god who created the world through his self-sacrifice while in the physical form of a boar. In many Eastern cultures, boars' tusks are prized as symbols of Vishnu's phallus, which mated with Mother Earth.

According to the Chinese zodiac, if you are born in the Year of the Boar, you are a noble and chivalrous person who will have lifelong friends.

A certain repugnance toward the boar passed into Christian tradition partly because of the old Jewish taboo against the eating of pork and partly because of the story of Jesus casting the legion of demons into the herd of swine at Gadarenes. On the other hand, the pig was the animal symbol of St. Anthony of Egypt.

If you can dissociate yourself from the centuries-old stigma of the pig as an unclean receptacle of demons, and remove yourself from the tired stereotype of the swine as a fat, greedy animal wallowing in a mud puddle, you can have a totem animal of remarkable power and strength. Deeply connected to the Earth Mother and the mysteries of nature, the boar will be able to guide you fearlessly through the trials and tribulations inherent on a human's lifepath.

By nature, the boar is a clean, well-organized creature that enjoys a mastery of its domain. As a totem animal, the boar can bring that same sense of self-reliance to you. You will be able to face life's problems knowing that you can emerge the conqueror.

**Bull, Buffalo**—As most readers of this book will already be aware, the magnificent animal that we call a buffalo is in reality a bison. We will yield to common nomenclature, however, and continue to refer to the Lord of the Plains as a buffalo.

In the early days of the United States, the buffalo ranged from the western plains to as far east as the Allegheny Mountains. Especially to the nomadic plains tribes, the buffalo was a living symbol of the perpetuation of their life force and their lifestyle. When the great one was slain, every part of its body was used, not a scrap wasted. The hunters and their families utilized the meat, the blood, the hide, the sinews, the horns, the hooves—and in some cases the slayer would kneel to breathe in the dying animal's breath.

Around the year 1822, an estimated 60 million buffalo roamed the plains. When the great slaughter of the animals began in the 1860s with the building of the railroad lines across the plains territories, the great Ogallala Teton Sioux Red Cloud took it as his mission from the Great Mystery to protect the buffalo.

When he began his war in 1865, the number of the buffalo had diminished to an estimated 13 million. Although Red Cloud won many important battles and even achieved the victory of preserving buffalo hunting grounds for his people, at the time of his death in 1909, the number of buffalo in the entire United States was estimated to be fewer than one thousand. Today, the spirit of Red Cloud may consider the comeback of the buffalo herds to be a mixed blessing, as they are now domesticated animals, rather than the free-roaming Lords of the Plains that they were in the past.

Although in the legend of the White Buffalo Woman the hunter's romantic feelings toward the enchantingly beautiful woman were rebuffed in a most violent manner, there are numerous accounts among Native American tribes of marriages between buffalo and humans. Other tales depict an underworld populated with buffalo that are awaiting a propitious time to reclaim the surface world.

Scholars of religion have long noted that sooner or later every primitive god becomes a bull. To the Egyptians, Apis, the sacred bull, annually sacrificed at Memphis, was a reflection of the Creator Spirit. Horus, the bull-calf, represents Osiris reborn from his mother, Isis-Hathor.

Bull worship was a central element in Mithraism, a cult that became popular throughout the Mediterranean region. Dionysus, an Orphic god, manifested in the form of a bull. In the apocryphal book of Enoch, the Messiah is represented as a white bull. In like manner, the great, charging form of the bull/buffalo was an impressive embodiment of the Great Mystery to those tribes whose continued existence depended upon its flesh.

Yama, the Hindu Lord of Death, has the head of a bull and judges the underworld. The Minotaur, in his labyrinthine caverns awaiting the foolhardy who seek to trespass in his domain, is another symbol of a guardian of the underworld, with the body of a man and the head of a bull.

Celtic representations of bulls, particularly those from Gaul, often depict the creature's mighty head with three horns, quite likely placing an emphasis on the horn as a power symbol.

The Irish feast of the bull, *tairbfeis*, included the drinking of the animal's blood, as well as the eating of its flesh. After thus eating and drinking, one might lie down to sleep on the bull's hide to have dreams of the future and the Other Side.

Grandmother Twylah of the Seneca teaches that the buffalo represents force and strength. If you should dream of a buffalo, you are being given a sign that you are supported by spirit in the accomplishment of a new project. If you often envision a buffalo, you are being given confidence in your ability to achieve your goals.

If you have chosen or accepted the buffalo as your totem animal, you have an ally that will encourage you to spend a great deal of time out-of-doors. Your buffalo totem will seek to help you establish a solid connection with the Earth Mother and will endeavor to teach you ways in which you may assist the many endangered creatures to avoid extinction. Your spirit helper will bring you strength of character and build within you an independent spirit that will prize freedom above all things.

**Butterfly**—The Greek word for both "soul" and "butterfly" is psyche, and it was once believed that human souls assumed the form of butterflies while they searched for a new incarnation. Throughout Europe, Asia, and the Americas, butterflies have maintained their standing as a symbol of the soul and rebirth.

To the Chinese, the butterfly is a symbol of joy and conjugal happiness. A Chinese bridegroom would endear himself to his new wife by presenting her with a jade butterfly, which represented the union of their souls.

In the butterfly's unique lifecycle from dead and dried chrysalis to vibrant and soaring entity, the early Christians found a ready symbol of the resurrection of the human soul and the resurrection of Christ. Certain Christian sects, however, perceived the lovely, but fragile, butterfly as a symbol of the transient and perishable nature of the flesh.

In the Dakota tradition, the butterfly represents the Door of the East, wherein appears the splendor of dawn, the dwelling place of the Great Mystery.

To other Native Americans, the butterfly was a living fragment of the rainbow, a beautiful creature that floats with soundless wings above wild flowers on sunny currents of air.

If the butterfly is your totem animal, you are probably a very lively person with rather exotic tastes who loves beautiful and colorful expressions of clothing, decor, art, poetry, music, and self. Although you are a high-energy person, you are also a visionary, so you have little difficulty in settling down in a quiet place in nature or in your own home and going deep into the Silence of meditation.

The butterfly totem will aid you in achieving depths of inner and outer exploration far beyond the ordinary. As a symbol of personal transformation, your spirit helper will hover ever-near to assist you in all those changes within yourself and within your environment that are necessary for you to attain the highest levels of enlightenment.

**Cat**—Perhaps no animal inspires such devotion and dedication—or such animosity and abhorrence—as the cat.

To the ancient Egyptians, the cat was accorded a place of reverence in both the home and the temple. A cemetery containing the mummies of thousands of black cats was unearthed in Egypt.

The popular folk belief that the cat possesses nine lives goes back to the Egyptian worship of Bast, the Cat-Mother goddess, who had nine incarnations, including that of the benevolent aspect of Hathor, the Lioness. The Egyptian word for cat was *Mau,* which is at once an imitation of the cat's call and the nearly universal human cry for Mama, mother. Cats came to be worshiped with such intensity in those ancient cities along the Nile that the wanton killing of a cat was punishable by death.

Bubastis, a city in Lower Egypt, dedicated itself to the worship of the cat. Each May some 700,000 pilgrims journeyed to the city to participate in a cat festival.

Because the old Egyptians had a great fear of the dark, they observed with awe that the cat, a nocturnal creature, walked the shadowed streets with the greatest of confidence. The ancient Egyptian sages made so much of the cat's midnight forays they declared that the cat alone was responsible for preventing the world from falling into eternal darkness.

On the other hand, in the old European tradition, the cat was accused of plotting to bring the world into the dark clutches of Satan. The cat, especially a black one, was regarded as the favorite familiar of the practitioners of dark and evil witchcraft. The Grand Inquisitors condemned nearly as many cats to the stake as witches. It is because of this baseless, old ecclesiastical judgment that the sighting of a black cat is said to be an omen of fast-approaching misfortune.

Whether people in the Middle Ages truly believed that the unwavering stare of a cat could cause demonic torments and even their deaths, an unreasoning fearful response to cats is known today as ailurphobia. The very sight of a cat would set Adolf Hitler trembling. Napoleon Bonaparte conquered nearly all of Europe, but if he should sight a cat in his palace, he shouted for help. Henry III of England would faint at the very appearance of a cat.

In ancient India, the cat was held sacred. A number of Sanskrit texts make many favorable references to the influence of the cat on humankind.

In Scandinavian countries, brides used to try their best to be married on Friday, the day of the goddess Freya. If a young woman married on a sunny Friday, it was certain that Freya, the cat-goddess of the Nordic people, would bless the union.

The domestic cat was, of course, unknown to the Native Americans until the advent of the European settler. Because of the creature's fondness for roaming at night, the Pueblos associated the cat with witchcraft, though this may also have been a result of the Spanish influence on their community.

If the cat is your totem animal, you have a spirit helper who is resourceful, strong, and fearless. You will experience a sense of confidence and a new feeling of courage will suffuse your being. You will find that you are no longer intimidated by any opposition that may be arrayed against you.

With the cat as your totem animal, you will be encouraged to express an agility in body and mind. You will be challenged to explore new vistas. Quite likely you were already a night person before you acquired the cat as your spirit helper, but if not, you will gain a new appreciation for the creative energy that can arrive after midnight.

Your spirit journeys will enable you to maintain a careful balance so that your emphasis on an independent lifestyle and a quest for mystical truths do not cause you to develop a taste for the bizarre and occult, which can tempt you to detour from the true spiritual goal of your lifepath.

**Cock/Rooster**—The crowing of the rooster at dawn is almost universally recognized as the official announcement that the Sun has banished darkness and returned to rule the day. The Sky Father has returned to his kingdom and all is well.

Ancient Roman soothsayers hailed the rooster as an entity that walked the line between light and darkness, between this world and the other. Hence, they drew omens from the manner in which the cock pecked scattered grains of wheat.

In the old Jewish tradition of atonement, the *Kapparah*, a rooster is killed, then passed around the head of the offender, as an offering to be accepted as a surrogate in his place.

In Europe during the Middle Ages, the rooster became a highly regarded Christian image; and it is during those dark decades that the rooster became a popular figure to be placed upon weather vanes, cathedral towers, and domes. The rooster looked always toward eternity to greet the Sun (i.e., Christ) as it rose in the East. The memory that it had been the crowing of the cock that reminded Peter he had betrayed his Lord three times contributed greatly to the symbol of the rooster as one ever vigilant to the subtle presence of evil. The Cock, thus, becomes the animal symbol of St. Peter and St. Vitus.

While the rooster is a symbol of the angel of dawn, who welcomes the new day, there is no denying the sexual prowess of the cock, as it struts proudly across the barnyard with its harem of hens. The instinct to defend both their territory and their many mates has been exploited down through the centuries by those who would transform them into fighting cocks for savage amusement and gambling.

In contemporary expressions of Santeria and Voodoo, the rooster is a favorite sacrifice to attract the favorable attention of the saintly spirits. The fact that *cock* is a common euphemism for the male sex organ adds to the fowl's appeal as a surrogate victim for the sacrificial knife.

For the Chinese, the rooster represents an enthusiastic and joyful approach to life, as well as a hearty sexual appetite. If you were born in the Year of the Cock, the Chinese zodiac acclaims you as someone with the pioneering spirit, devoted to work and a quest for knowledge.

If the rooster is your totem animal, you may find it directing you to the more simple and basic pleasures of life. While on one level your totem animal represents an earthy pride in its own physical prowess, it also encourages a deeper exploration of the mysteries of the Other Side. As your spirit helper, the rooster may well suggest that you begin to study your dreams for prophetic insight into the dawn of new days.

**Condor**—The journal of an early Roman Catholic priest records that the first time the Native American members of his California mission saw the representation of the dove over the altar, they asked if it was the Black Coats' thunderbird.

The great condor of the Andes is the thunderbird of the native peoples of that area. Just before Sherry and I formed a circle of light in a sacred ancient Peruvian site, we offered our blessings as visiting Children of the Eagle (the United States) to the Children of the Condor (the Incas and their descendants among the contemporary Peruvians). Receiving our goodwill was an able young Shaman's apprentice named Kuichy (Rainbow), who said that the presence of the great condor soaring high above the tallest peaks in the Andes is an ever-present reminder that the Incas of old will one day return to Earth from their home in the stars.

If your totem spirit is a condor, you will be certain to be guided to unexpected heights of awareness. There is much power in this totem animal, so you must prepare yourself for its wisdom with much time spent in meditation. The condor is a wise spirit that will insist upon you developing your own potential as a counselor and guide to other humans.

Although you will be tempted to spend all of your time soaring higher and higher to new and unexplored levels of consciousness, your condor totem animal will insist that you focus equal amounts of time developing your physical body and your mental acuity.

**Cougar**—Depending upon where you live in the United States, the great, tawny mountain lion is called a cougar, panther, or puma. While the cougar once ranged throughout most of North America, the animal's kingdom is now largely restricted to the southwest.

According to an old story, which may be apocryphal, the cougar was christened a "mountain lion" when early European traders believed the tawny pelts the tribesmen were swapping to be the hides of female lions, such as the ones that they had seen in Africa. When they asked the native hunters why they brought in only female pelts for trade, the whimsical tribesmen, seeking to play a joke on the naive white men, said that the male lions were so fierce that they lived all by themselves far up in the mountains.

To the tribes of North America, the cougar is the master of the hunt, the creature whose prowess in bringing down game is unsurpassed. Its method of quietly watching and slowly stalking its prey provided a model of caution and subtlety for the hunter. As one chant in honor of the cougar says it, *Now I am come up out of the ground/I am ruler of the season.*

Considered the Elder Brother by many North American tribes, the cougar was imbued with many mystical qualities. Its eyes became globes of fire at night. Its scream in the darkness could paralyze a deer or an unwary human. Its wisdom and Medicine would be shared with those spiritual seekers who approached it with the proper reverence and purity of heart.

According to the Native American zodiac, those born from February 19 to March 20 are under the sign of the cougar. Cougar people are described as sensitive, easily hurt by disapproval or rejection, and highly mystical in nature.

If you have the cougar as a totem animal, you are likely the kind of individual who enjoys exploring the mystical side of life. While you may be thoroughly domestic in one part of your nature, you know that you also harbor within a wild, primitive aspect that could be unleashed at inopportune moments. There is a part of you that could relish running off and getting lost in the wilderness. There is a hidden element within your psyche that dreams of racing through the forest in the dark, of dancing around a campfire, of living in a much simpler time. Your cougar guide will help you attain a balance between the ancient memories of a faraway and long ago time for which a part of you yearns and the here and now in which the present you must successfully adapt and flourish.

Your cougar totem can bring out a certain aggressive streak within you, but your spirit voyages can assure you that you become a hunter of dreams and visions, rather than a hunter of another entity's blood and lifeforce. Rather than striking out in anger and revenge, you will learn to speak out in peace and love.

**Cow**—The vital importance of the bovine in the evolution of humankind has often been glorified in the passionate deification of cattle. Because the cow has always been associated with both the earth and the moon, numerous lunar goddesses wear the horns of the cow upon their heads. (Think of how that old nursery rhyme about the cow jumping over the moon perpetuates a spiritual symbol that has survived for centuries.)

Asherah, the Semitic name of the Great Goddess mentioned in the Old Testament, was represented as the Heavenly Cow. The Golden Calf, whose worship so upset Moses, was Horus-Ra, the child of the Great Mother Hathor, the divine cow of Egypt.

The Norse said that the world was created by the body and blood of the giant Ymir, but it was acknowledged that the Great Mother Cow had to precede him, for he subsisted on her milk.

Buana, the Good Mother of the Irish, was presented in the image of a cow, whose flowing milk represented wealth and a time of plenty. The cow is also the animal associated with Brigid, an Irish saint.

The entire continent of Europe is named after Europa, the white moon cow who was mated with Zeus, King of the Gods, in his incarnation as a white bull.

The ancient Indians went even farther in their tribute to the Great Mother Cow. They believed that the entire planet was created by the churning of a great sea of milk that curdled into solid lumps. The milk-giving cow remains sacred in India to this day, revered as a symbol of Kali.

The Japanese also adhered to the curdle theory of creation. Various deities vigorously stirred the sea of mother's milk until clumps of land began to appear.

If the cow is your totem animal, you are quite likely a warm and nurturing person who cares deeply about your family, your community, and the global environment. The concept of a herd that functions as a cooperative unit may appeal to you on many levels.

While you may have been a gentle, passive, largely unassertive person in the past, the cow as your totem animal will teach you how to be lovingly assertive. Do not judge your spirit helper by the sleepy-eyed, cud-chewing, passive creatures that you view in a farmer's pasture. The essence of the cow as a spirit guide is the powerful mother vibration that eternally nurtures, but who also accepts the maternal responsibility of chastisement and discipline.

This totem helper can teach you a great deal in this new age of the female, but you must assume your responsibility of spending respectful time in the Silence so that you may truly learn and grow.

**Coyote**—The Coyote holds a most unique place in the legends and folklore of North American tribes. Although intimately associated with the Great Mystery in the very act of creation, his wily descendants are both pests and relentless competitors in the serious business of survival on the Earth Mother.

One of the tribes of old California believed that the coyotes were the first humans who ever existed. In the beginning, of course, they walked on all fours. Then, gradually, they began to grow certain human body parts—a finger here, a toe there, an ear here. Over the course of generations, they eventually became perfect humans with beautiful tails. Although the tails were handsome, they slowly wore away through the human habit of sitting upright.

To another southwestern tribe, the coyote became an early, godlike savior of humankind. Originally, so goes the old legend, the Great Sun Chief had nine brothers, all flaming hot like himself. The native people down on Mother Earth were about to wither and die under the terrible heat of ten suns burning down on them. Brother Coyote, quickly assessing the situation and immediately perceiving the answer, leaped into the sky and slew the Sun Chief's fiery brothers, thus saving the tribespeople from baking to a crisp.

However, this problem had no sooner been solved when Sister Moon's nine sisters, each as cold as she, began to turn the night into a freezing torment. Once again, the tribespeople were helpless, for they had no way to keep warm, and they appealed to Brother Coyote to help them lest they perish.

Coyote had to have time to think, so he retreated to the far eastern edge of the world. After a time, the Great Mystery sent him an idea. Coyote picked up his flint knife and struck it against a rock. Sparks flew into some leaves, and almost before he knew it, he had created fire. He took a few moments to warm his paws over the flames, then leaped into the sky and slew each of Sister Moon's frigid sisters, thus saving humankind from freezing to death. But as an aid to their keeping warm on cold winter nights, Coyote gave the tribes the gift of fire.

So it was the coyote who gave humankind the knowledge of how to make fire, how to grind flour, and how to find the herbs that would bring about the quickest cures. But Brother Coyote has a very strange temperament—or maybe he didn't think he received enough thanks for his gifts—for he is also a Trickster. True, he brought fire and food and healing herbs to humankind, but he also brought death. The tribespeople soon learned that when you ask such a creature to grant you a wish, you had better hope that there will not be some twist attached to it.

Medicine teachers Star-Spider Woman and Rattling Bear caution that if you must be foolish enough to ask Coyote a favor, at least be very precise in what you request.

The Navajo regard the coyote as the very essence, sign, and symbol of Dark Side witchcraft. If a Navajo were to set out on a journey and spot a coyote crossing his path, he would go home and wait for three days before setting out again. Borrowing the devil from the Christian missionaries, the Navajo believe that Satan uses the coyote as his steed on evil nocturnal missions.

If you have received the coyote as your totem animal, you must first remove all negative connotations from your mind about the creature being a representative of the Dark Side of spirit. The coyote is an exceedingly resourceful animal with amazing powers of adaptability. Listen carefully to your coyote totem guide, for it will teach you the fine line between wisdom and folly.

The coyote totem spirit may well have come to you because you, too, are a survivor, a person who knows how to adapt to any situation, good or bad. Ancient wisdom lies within the vibration of this spirit helper, but to gain its greatest spiritual treasures, you must truly pay very careful attention to the essence of each and every message that your guide relays to you. This totem animal will teach you discernment, one of the most valuable of all survival lessons on the earthplane.

**Crab**—In the lore of Tahiti, the crab is the symbol of the god of fugitives, since it can be seen scurrying from rock to rock as it heads for the sea, trying its best to escape the scrutiny and detection of its natural predators.

There is an old Japanese folktale of feuding families that battled so fiercely that the losers, in their humiliation, threw themselves into the sea, rather than face disgrace on land. Once they sank to the bottom of the ocean, however, they were not drowned, but were transformed into crabs.

Ancient Chaldean astrologers believed that the world would end and disintegrate into its primordial elements when all the planets were lined up in the constellation of the Crab. Because the wisdom of the Chaldeans was honored by astrologers in other cultures, their apocalyptic prophecy was given great credence in Egypt, India, Persia, China, and Europe.

In the zodiac, the sign of the Crab is from June 22 to July 22. Those born under this sign are sometimes said to be imaginative, but somewhat lacking in willpower. Home is very important to Crab people and they guard its sanctity with great determination.

If the crab has come to you as a totem animal through your dreams or visions, you might examine your personal life to see if you have a tendency to hold on to things that would better be released. This spirit helper comes to you from the water, a symbol of the unconscious, and it will aid you in determining what elements within your life need to be set free in order to elevate your consciousness to higher planes of awareness.

This totem animal will also help you to increase your powers of endurance and to develop a harder shell around your sensitive nature. Learn to listen to this spirit helper's advice as to when to hold on and when to let go of certain challenges and opportunities.

**Crow/Raven**—This large, stately black bird assumes an almost universal role as a symbol of death or destiny.

Among the Celtic people, the bird was associated with various war goddesses, who could assume the form of a raven at will. The Vikings held similar beliefs about the valkyries, and it was decreed that understanding the speech of birds could help one gain entry to the world of valkyries and ravens, where the results of future battles were ordained. Valkyries, in their coats of lustrous black feathers, were also known as *Kraken,* or crows. Warriors who fell in battle and whose bodies could not be reclaimed by friends or family were known as *hrafengrennir,* "raven feeders."

The great Danish hero Sigurd was the son of King Ragnar Lodbrok and the valkyrie Krake, a shape-shifter who could choose to be a beautiful maiden or a crow.

In numerous fairy tales of the northern Europeans, the raven is the spirit helper who guides the hero through the dangerous turns and traps of his quest. The raven is also a reliable consultant on the vagaries of the Other World.

In the Germanic tradition, the great hero Emperor Frederick is guarded by ravens as he sleeps in his underground sanctuary until the day of his return to earth.

During the dark and troubled Middle Ages in Europe, the crow also came to be associated with Satan because of its black color and raucous cry. Moralistic animal fables were told of the crow's shame of its blackness, even to the point of scattering mud on elegant swans in an attempt to make them look like him. They, of course, could wash off the dirt, but the jealous crow could never change his color. St. Antony, however, was not disturbed by such negative reports against the crow, for he chose it as his animal symbol.

Among many Native American tribes, especially among the plains and southwestern groups, the crow is a trickster figure, similar in many ways to the coyote.

The Dakota envision the crow as an assistant to the plover, the Spirit of the South, who presided over warm weather. When the Spirit of the North arrived with his winter wolves, a battle ensued between them and the crow and the plover. According to tradition, if the two birds with their war clubs are able to beat back the wolves, warm weather would prevail for a little while longer before the harsh cold set in over the plains.

The Pueblo groups usually associate owls and crows with Dark Side witchcraft, and it was generally accepted that witches could change themselves into crows at will and fly at night to work their evil deeds.

In the Native American zodiac, those born from September 23 to October 22 are Crow/Raven people. The Medicine Wheel describes them as social, energetic, and full of nervous energy and fluctuating moods. But they are generally very flexible and adapt well to new environments and circumstances.

If you have selected the crow as your totem animal—or if the crow has selected you—you may consider yourself to be something of a shape-shifter, gifted at wearing many faces. Be cautious of becoming too manipulative of others and impinging upon the free will of those who may be a bit gullible and easily led.

Your crow is a keen-eyed student of the environment from a perspective seldom achieved by ordinary observers. As one who watches shrewdly over the lay of the land on both spiritual and physical levels, your totem animal expresses a point of view that touches several dimensions. As you learn better how to listen, you will find that he is a messenger without peer.

As a spirit helper, the crow will be able to get you in touch with many ancient mysteries, but you must regularly enter the Silence to be certain that you do not yield to the temptation of exploiting the powers of these ancient wisdoms for the glory of the Dark Side. If you are able to maintain your spiritual balance, the crow will guide you to become a gifted practitioner of True Magick and Medicine.

**Dog**—For the Celtic people, the dog, horse, and bull were considered the three most important domestic animals with a sacred significance. Throughout most of northern Europe, the dog was associated with various mother goddesses. It was commonplace to bury a great leader with his pack of dogs, and for the Irish, both the wolf and the hunting dog were used as symbols of accomplished young warriors.

A warrior society of the Cheyenne called themselves the Dog Soldiers, or Crazy Dogs, and vowed never to retreat in battle, regardless of the fierceness of the fray or how badly they might be outnumbered.

Artemis/Diana, the classical mythological figure of the Goddess of the Hunt, manifested for the evening's pursuit of game surrounded by her pack of dogs. The powerful goddess figure of the huntress is replicated in Sarama, the Vedic mother of the Dogs of Yama, and the Hounds of Annwn, the Celtic goddess.

The Scandinavians portrayed the dog as the guardian of the underworld; thus, it was customary to bury a dog with the deceased as a guide to the afterlife. In their cosmology, it will be the hound Garm that will set in motion the events leading to Ragnarok, earth's fiery end, and it will be the wolf Fenrir that will break loose at the time of destruction.

A number of the eastern Native American tribes also believed that a dog was stationed to guard the Way of the Departed Spirits.

The ancient Egyptian's Anubis, the dog-headed god, is also a canine gatekeeper of the Other World, responsible for admitting souls to paradise. Hecate, the Goddess of Death, is portrayed always attended by dogs, her animal totems. Her most fierce, Cerberus, the three-headed hound, is set to guard the gates to her underworld kingdom.

An old Semitic tradition states that the Angel of Death can only be seen by dogs, which is why, the old tales say, dogs howl at the moon to announce a death.

English folklore has the ominous legend of the Black Dog, a beast whose appearance presages doom, death, or, at best, despair. There is also a legend of a benevolent Black Dog, who appears to guide travelers to a safe haven.

If you were born during the Year of the Dog, the Chinese zodiac describes you as a generous, loyal, honest person who works well with people.

The Inuits have a legend of the Dog People—not to be confused with the Cheyenne Dog Soldiers—the offspring of a great red dog and an Inuit woman. This beast marriage produced five ugly monsters and five dogs, and the disgusted mother set them all adrift on rafts. The five dogs reached the shores of Europe and begat among them the white people. The monsters evolved into horrible, bloodthirsty cannibals who still haunt the northern icelands.

No less than five Christian saints have the dog as their animal symbol. Of course there is St. Bernard, but there are also St. Dominic, St. Roch, St. Eustace, and St. Hubert.

According to Grandmother Twylah, the traditional Seneca see the dog as representing fidelity and devotion, the symbol of a friend who is always available whenever he or she is truly needed.

If you have discovered the dog to be your totem animal, it is quite likely that you prize dependability, loyalty, and faithfulness as primary virtues in your selection of friends. You will certainly be able to expect such strong allegiance from your dog totem. Whenever this spirit helper is near, you will feel strong emanations of love surrounding you.

With the dog as your totem animal, you will also experience a strong sense of being protected and watched over, night and day.

This spirit helper will be a dependable guide in your explorations of higher consciousness, and you may rely on it always to warn you of any impending threat from Dark Side entities. You are certain to feel its comfortable vibration near you as you enter the Silence to gain deeper wisdom teachings.

**Deer**—Among all Native American tribes who had contact with the deer, the graceful creature was considered a sacred totemic animal. The Medicine doctors of various tribes believed that the deer had a keen sense of determining which plants yielded the greatest curative powers, and a great deal of time was spent stalking the deer for its ostensible knowledge of pharmacology as well as its flesh.

The Native American zodiac names deer people as those born from May 21 to June 21 and says that they are generally of a good disposition, but they sometimes appear to be creatures of perpetual motion.

In numerous cultures throughout Europe, Asia, and North America, the male deer, the stag, was regarded as a symbol of regeneration because of the way its antlers are renewed. In certain mystical traditions, the horned deer is also linked with the Tree of Life because of the similarity between its antlers and the branches of a tree. Consequently, the horn contained great magic, whether worn intact, broken in pieces, or ground into powder.

Very early in humankind's religious observations, the stag became the Shamans' Horned God, the sacrificial consort of such goddesses as the huntress Diana/Artemis. With the spread of Christianity across Europe, the Horned God easily became a representation of Satan; but in nearly as many instances, the stag was idealized as a symbol of Christ, for the deer, as did Jesus on the cross, gave its blood (flesh) for humankind. St. Withburga has the doe, the female deer, as her animal symbol.

If the deer has come to you as your totem animal or if you have felt drawn to the animal through a dream or a vision, your spirit self is now in the company of one who has long been cherished as an intermediary between the Great Mystery and humankind. With the deer as your totem, you will feel an acceleration of your powers of intuition. Many Shamans attribute the greatest psychic sensitivity to the Deer People.

With the deer as your spirit helper, you will find that you have an increased desire to spend more time in the Silence and in nature. You will also notice that your dreams have become more enriched. Among the lore of some native tribes is a regard for the deer as the Lord of the Dream. To focus on the deer before falling asleep, according to some, will bring prophetic dreams that may be shared for the good of your family and/or your community.

**Dolphin**—Demeter, the ancient Greek goddess of fertility, chose the dolphin as her totem animal, thus representing her position as Mistress of the Sea. The serpent symbolized her majesty as Mistress of the Earth.

Since the earliest days of sea lore, dolphins have been credited with saving the lives of shipwrecked humans. In both old Roman and early Christian art, the dolphin was depicted as the guide that would bear souls of the dead across the waters to the Blessed Isles.

For Mediterranean Christians, the dolphin, King of the Fishes, came to represent Christ, King of Heaven. A rather common Christian image was that of the dolphin together with an anchor, representing salvation firmly anchored on faith in Christ.

For the Native American tribes located on coastal regions frequented by the dolphin, the aquatic mammal was identified as a special messenger of the Great Mystery.

If the dolphin is your totem animal, you are allied with a spirit helper that has come to you from another realm of being. There is a playfulness associated with this totem animal that can be misleading for those who would be satisfied with superficial teachings. Always ask this spirit helper to take you deeper and deeper into the mysteries of the other realm from which it originates.

You will quite likely find that the dolphin will increase your respect and love for all living things and assist you in developing new levels of compassion. Be prepared to begin looking at the world from a very different perspective as your "dolphin eyes" consider all beings around you as elements in universal harmony.

**Dove**—In the ancient and classical worlds, the dove was associated with such goddesses as Aphrodite and Astarte and considered a symbol of sexual passion. In India, the dove was a symbol of lust, the *paravata.* It was the dove that bore the ambrosia from the goddesses that kept Father Zeus immortal.

The Pleiades, the Seven Sisters in the night sky, were also known in Greece as "a flock of doves," the daughters of Aphrodite.

Sophia, the Goddess of Wisdom, descended upon her chosen human vessels in the form of a dove. In various traditions, including Gnostic Christianity, Sophia represented the female soul of God, the source of his power.

Xochiquetzal, in the legends of old Mexico, is a combination of love goddess and madonna, who becomes the mother of all races after a great flood. Taking pity on her human progeny, who lack the gift of speech, her spirit in the form of a dove descends upon them and creates the languages of the world.

In the Hebrew tradition, the dove became a symbol of peace and innocence when it returned to Noah's ark with the olive branch from the Mount of Olives in its beak. The dove is also used an image of the *shekhinah,* or Divine Presence.

The dove is a common symbol of the Holy Spirit in Christian and Muslim traditions. It was as a dove that the Holy Spirit descended on Mary to proclaim her blessed among women and on Jesus at the time of his baptismal rite at the hands of John the Baptist. A dove fell from Mohammad's ear, thus convincing his followers that he was receiving guidance directly from the Holy Spirit. In Christian folklore, the dove is considered so holy that even Satan, the most accomplished shape-shifter of all, cannot disguise himself in its image.

Four Christian saints are identified with the dove—St. Ambrose, St. David, St. Gregory, and St. Samson.

Among many Native American tribes, the dove is thought to be the form that the dead may take immediately after their transition from flesh to spirit. The feathers of the dove were often used on prayer sticks.

If the dove is your totem spirit, you may have been a troubled and angry individual who needed an infusion of peace in your life. On the other hand, you may have been a person who has been devoted to bringing about peace, love, and harmony to the best of your mortal ability. In either case, your spirit helper will bring the infusion of sacred energy that you require to assist you in accomplishing your mission and purpose on the Earth Mother.

This totem spirit can also assist you in establishing a more secure love relationship with your lover or spouse. By focusing on its energy, you will find yourself becoming more at ease around members of the opposite sex and more responsive to their moods and emotions.

As a spirit teacher, the dove can move you back through the mists of time to absorb the ancient wisdoms and help you to apply these essential truths to your contemporary problems. As a guide on your spirit journeys, your dove totem will always see to it that all goes smoothly and harmoniously.

**Donkey/Ass**—Ancient people revered the ass because it was so important for their survival. Rather easily domesticated, wherever the beast of burden was found throughout the world, it was highly esteemed as a faithful friend to humankind.

In India, the sacred king Ravana had ten crowned human heads surmounted by the head of an ass. In ancient Egypt, the ass was a symbol of the sun god, Ra. Set, one of the Egyptian dynastic gods, bore the head of an ass on his shoulders, and his kingly scepter flourished a pair of ass's ears at its tip. In Greece, the animal was considered sacred to Dionysus.

The mighty Hebrew hero Samson slew the Philistines with the jawbone of an ass. And after Jesus entered Jerusalem on Palm Sunday on the colt of an ass, the sturdy four-legged beast was held sacred by the Christians. According to an old folk legend, the dark cross of hair across the donkey's shoulders was thought to be an everlasting reminder of its role in the passion of Christ.

If the ass, the donkey, is your totem animal, your spirit helper may have assessed as one of your basic needs the necessity of getting down to serious business regarding your mission on the earthplane. You may also discover that you are becoming much more conscientious about the small details that you may previously have tended to ignore, and that you are learning to be more practical and goaloriented in your various earthly pursuits.

The donkey also comes to the workaholic and cautions against too much work and not enough time wisely spent in recreation, family activities, and spiritual searching. As a spirit helper, the donkey will present you with solid, sensible advice on your quest to higher awareness.

**Duck**—The Native American tribes of the northeast admired the duck as a marvelously resilient individual. In tribute to the hardy fowl is the tale of Shingebiss, who dared to defy the very spirit of the north wind.

Shingebiss lived alone in his lodge, hardy and fearless. He would venture out on even the coldest days, find a hole in the ice, and dive into the water for his fish. In this way, he always had plenty to eat while others, less hardy, were nearly famished. While they sat in their lodges nearly starving because they did not dare brave the cold, Shingebiss could be seen returning home with strings of fish.

Kabibonokka, the spirit of the north wind, had watched the boldness of the little duck with growing annoyance. How dare the feathered fisher ignore even the most severe of his icy blasts? To teach the duck a lesson, Kabibonokka sent forth tenfold colder blasts and drifts of snow, so that it was nearly impossible for any creature to live in the open. But still, Shingebiss went about his daily fishing, seemingly unmindful of the terrible cold.

The spirit of the north wind decided to pay a visit to the duck in his lodge. There he found Shingebiss happily frying fish over his fire. Kabibonokka entered the lodge, anticipating that his very presence would turn the duck to ice. But Shingebiss merely built up the fire until Kabibonokka could no longer bear the heat and fled his lodge.

As Kabibonokka left the lodge, he heard the duck chanting: "Windy god, blow your coldest breeze / Shingebiss you cannot freeze. / Ho, for life! Ho, for bliss. / Who is so free as Shingebiss?"

At last the spirit of the north wind gave up. "He must be aided by some powerful manitou," Kabibonokka said. "I can neither freeze nor starve him. I think he is a very wonderful being. I will let him alone."

If the duck is your totem animal, be advised that just as the physical representation of its energy swims upon the water of lakes and ponds, so does the spirit representation of its energy swim and dive into the pool of creative energy hidden in your subconscious. The duck will also assist you in building emotional stability and will enable you to face daily challenges with a stronger emotional balance. Just as their physical counterparts bravely navigate through the stormy waters of their often hostile environment, so will the spirit essence of the duck help you to find your way through the sometimes rough emotional wave of your physical environment.

Interestingly, just as contemporary artists and storytellers have often depicted the duck as an amusing and daffy character, your spirit helper will also teach you to be able to laugh at yourself and to discover the strength in a good sense of humor.

**Eagle**—Among ancient Mediterranean people, the eagle was associated with the sun god, fire, and lightning. Zeus, the father of the classical gods, took the form of an eagle when he carried his young lover Ganymede to Mt. Olympus.

For the Romans, the eagle became a symbol of the sovereignty of its emperors, and the image was carried before the Empire's legions as they set about conquering the known world.

The eagle became a popular symbol of power among the Germanic people because the great bird was representative of Wodan, the ruler of the gods. As with the Romans before them with their Caesars, the eagle's mastery of the heavens came to symbolize the sovereignty of the German kaisers.

Because the eagle could appear to fly so close to the sun, the Medicine priests of all the tribes regarded the large bird as a very special messenger of the Great Mystery.

In India, the Vedic tradition also portrays the eagle as a messenger of divinity and as the bearer of *soma,* the favorite drink of the Vedic gods, from Indra.

An old Aztec folktale tells of the *ciuapipiltin,* spirits of women who died in childbirth, who returned to earth to snare the children of living mothers. These entities could appear in the form of ghostly women or as an eagle, swooping down from the sky.

Psalms 103:5, "so that thy youth is renewed like an eagle's"; and Isaiah 40:31, "They that wait upon the Lord shall renew their strength; they shall mount up with wings as eagles," both allude to the old Hebrew belief that the eagle had the ability to plunge into the sea and regenerate itself every ten years.

Over the years in Christian iconography, the eagle has represented a special messenger from Heaven, the spirit of prophecy, a prayer rising swiftly to God, and even the Ascension of Christ. St. John the Evangelist is identified with the eagle.

In the old days, eagle feathers were used whenever possible on Native American war bonnets, rattles, shields, pipes, baskets, prayer sticks, and all kinds of ceremonial costumes. The very style in which the feathers were clipped, colored, and arranged on a chief's or warrior's clothing would reveal his rank in the tribe and the deeds that he had accomplished to earn that rank. Today, of course, with the eagle on the endangered species list, pseudo-eagle feathers are created from crow, chicken, and turkey feathers.

And speaking of turkeys, if Ben Franklin had had his way, the turkey would be the official fowl of the United States, rather than the bald eagle. Franklin considered the eagle to be little more than a scavenger, while in his opinion, the turkey was an honest, decent bird.

The origin of placing such high esteem on eagle feathers was told in an old Native American folktale that recounts how all the birds met one day to decide once and for all which could fly the highest. Some flew up very swiftly, but soon became tired, but the eagle flew beyond them all and was about to claim the victory when the crafty gray linnet suddenly emerged from its hiding place on the eagle's back and, fresh and rested, succeeded in flying the highest.

When the birds came back to alight on the Earth Mother, the great council of fowls still voted to award the prize to the eagle, for not only had it flown closer to the sun than the other birds, it had done so with the linnet on its back. Hence, from that day forward, the feathers of the eagle were esteemed the most honorable adornment for the warrior, as it is not only the bravest bird, but it is also endowed with strength to soar the highest.

If the eagle has appeared to you in your dreams or visions and revealed itself as your totem animal, you may expect to receive renewed strength of body, mind, and spirit. At the same time, you will find your meditations becoming more profound and your visions more prophetic in content. If you maintain a harmonious and balanced lifestyle, you will feel a stronger connection with the Great Mystery than ever before in your spiritual pilgrimage on earth.

Just as the eagle can soar high above the earth and rise above its companions and its competitors, you must guard against the powerful eagle vibrations causing you to withdraw from your family and friends and grow aloof from your community. If you listen carefully to your spirit helper, it will instruct you in the sacred responsibility of sharing your prophetic insights with others and show you how to become the most effective kind of spiritual teacher.

**Elephant**—If the United States is Turtle Island, a continent supported on the back of a turtle, then India would be Elephant Island, a continent supported on the back of an elephant. Throughout the centuries, Indian tradition dictated that all royalty, the rulers of the land, be borne on the backs of the children of the great beast that carried the world through space.

The elephant was the totem animal of the god Shiva, the Destroyer, who seeks to banish illusion and to encourage a clearer perception of reality. Shiva and his goddess-spouse, Radha, produced among their children the elephant-headed god Ganesha, who, as Lord of Hosts, impregnated the virgin Maya to bring Buddha into flesh.

Especially sacred in India was the white elephant, considered far too priceless to be used for work or warfare, but to be maintained by its owner in the finest of style. When we speak today of a "white elephant" purchase, we have realized too late that we have purchased an object at a price that exceeds its true value.

Sometimes seen as a symbol of great sexual prowess in the Asian countries, the Chinese portray the elephant as representative of royalty, strength of purpose, and discretion.

In the widest, most universal, and most obvious depiction of the elephant, it is a symbol of strength. At various times in Medieval Europe, the elephant also became an emblem of wisdom, moderation, and eternity. Then, accomplishing a complete change of cosmology, there appeared the elephant-headed demon, Behemoth, a favorite in Dark Side sorcery.

If you have accepted the elephant as your totem animal, it may not be long before you are asked to assume a role of great responsibility in the workplace or in your community. If you feel attracted to the elephant as a totem animal, it is likely that you are involved in social work, public service, or politics. You may also feel a strong commitment to caring for the ill, the very young, and the elderly.

Whenever you sense an injustice, you will be there on the side of the underdog.

As your spirit helper, the elephant will be able to draw you back to a greater appreciation for the ancient mysteries than you have previously experienced. You will soon discover that your guide is extremely concerned about your maintaining always a solid balance of body, mind, and spirit. Under the tutelage of this spirit helper, you will place your time in the Silence as your top priority. You might find yourself wishing to burn some incense while you are meditating with this totem animal in order to help create an environment in which exploration of other higher levels of consciousness will be the rule, rather than the exception.

**Falcon**—To the ancient Egyptians, the falcon-headed god was Horus, son of Isis, whose left eye became the moon and whose right eye became the sun, thus enabling him to watch over his human charges night and day.

Many Native American tribes believed that the falcon possessed special insight into the workings of the Great Mystery and that they were somehow intimately associated with human destiny. The Italian poet Dante must have been similarly inspired when he wrote in his masterpiece, *The Divine Comedy*, of the "celestial falcons" that drove off the evil snake so the angels could return to their stations watching over humankind.

Native people on the eastern coast of Peru have a creation myth that tells of five falcon eggs left high on a mountaintop in the Andes that hatched into the Creator and his brother, the four winds.

If the falcon has come to you in a dream or a vision and presented itself to you as your totem animal, you may have a very strong independent spirit. It is likely that you prize your solitude and enjoy spending long hours just walking in nature. You may already be quite adept at going deep into the Silence of meditation.

This particular spirit helper will be very loyal to you and very respectful of your earthwalk to higher awareness. You may expect to experience a number of extremely significant astral, or out-of-body, journeys to other dimensions of reality. Your falcon guide will fly with you to astonishing recreations of the past and remarkable projections of the future—all of which will aid you in creating positive applications for more successful achievements in the present.

**Fish**—Fish constituted one of the basic food items for many Native American tribes.

As a universal symbol, the fish is highly revered by numerous cultures. To many native people, the fish serves as a symbol of hidden knowledge, for it dives deeply to explore the unknown depths of the waters.

The fish was sacred to the Babylonians, Phoenicians, and Assyrians, and it was also esteemed as an emblem of fertility. In Scandinavia, the Goddess Freya's day was Friday, a day devoted to lovemaking. Fish, considered to be an aphrodisiac by the old Norse, were consumed in large quantities that day by hopeful lovers. The Celts also believed that a meal of fish could aid a couple in conceiving a child.

The early Christians adopted the sign of the fish as a symbol of Christ, for the Greek *ichthys* provided them with an acronym for "Jesus Christ, Son of God."

There are, of course, many kinds of fish, but it can be said in a general way that if an entity of the lakes or streams should come to you as a spirit animal, you may expect to be put in touch with many basic elements in nature that you may previously have ignored or given little attention. As a creature of the waters, this spirit helper will also represent to your deeper levels of consciousness a willingness to develop new expressions of creativity.

If a fish has presented itself to you in a dream or a vision, you may be about to experience a bit of good fortune in the workplace. A dream of hauling in a good catch of fish can also presage a positive turn in your personal relationship with a member of the opposite sex.

If a fish has come to you as a spirit helper, be open to exploring ancient mysteries that will reveal an astonishing perspective of the Earth Mother, from primordial seas to soaring spaceships.

**Fox**—In the traditions of many Native American tribes, the fox is often associated with Dark Side witchcraft, and it is further believed that the sleek form of the fox is often favored as an image of trans-formation by a shape-shifting sorcerer or negative practitioner of Medicine Power.

In Europe, the fox was the essence of wiliness, quick-wittedness, and canny wisdom. In the Middle Ages, a popular folk hero was Reynard the Fox, a sly, picaresque hero, who always manages to over-come the brute strength and numbers of his adversaries by his clev-erness.

A favorite Japanese folktale tells of Abe No Yasuna, a poet and hero, who rescued a white fox from a hunting party and set it free. Not long after, he fell in love with the lovely Kuzunhoa, who re-turned his affection and agreed to marry him. Tragically, however, a year later she died giving birth to their son, Abe No Seimei, who would one day become magician and astrologer to the Emperor. Three days after Kuzunhoa's death, however, she came to her griev-ing husband in a dream and confessed that she had been the white fox that he had so nobly saved.

If the fox has presented itself to you as your totem animal in a dream or a vision, you have gained an ally that is truly a survivor. This spirit helper will bring a quickening of your physical and mental responses to any problem that you may have to face in your chosen quest on the lifepath, and you will also discover that your intuitive abilities have increased.

It is likely that you are a "night person," preferring to accomplish your mental tasks and your most important creative work while oth-ers are asleep. Acquiring the fox as your totem helper will probably only accentuate your normal nocturnal habits and, at the same time, prompt some extraordinary dream teachings when at last you do go to bed. Having a bit of the trickster in its nature, your spirit teacher will undoubtedly employ a great deal of challenging symbolism in your dreams and visions. Be assured that the benefits to be gained from cracking these hidden messages will be well worth the extra ef-fort, for the fox is a master teacher.

**Frog**—The frog is a very ancient symbol of rebirth. In old Egypt, Hekat, Queen of the Heavenly Midwives, wore a sacred amulet in the shape of a frog that bore the inscription, "I am the Resurrection."

To the ancient Romans, the frog was sacred to Venus, the love goddess. The frog as a popular fertility symbol goes all the way back to Babylon.

During the Middle Ages in Europe, Hekat had become Hecate, Queen of the Ghostworld or Queen of the Witches, and her frog totem had become a familiar that allegedly set curses and spells on the unwary.

Because of its amphibious nature, in many systems of magic the frog represents the transition from earth to water and vice versa. Add to this its largely nocturnal activities, and the frog becomes a totem animal favored by moon goddesses and other night creatures.

Early scientists mused that more than any other of the "cold-blooded" animals, the frog appeared to be a transitional step toward humans. Perhaps this line of thinking encouraged the fairy tales that tell of transforming a frog into a prince or princess or vice versa through the magic of a virginal kiss.

A West African folktale attributes the advent of death into the world to the frog, who reached the gods with his decree that humans should not be immortal before the faithful dog got to them with his plea that humans should have eternal life.

For many North American tribes, the frog was the great rain-maker of spring, summer, and fall. During the winter months, the people of the northeastern tribes began to worry about how the little manitous were faring under the ice. A Chippewa folksong by a poet of long ago imagines the plight of the *Okogies* (frogs) as they found themselves crying out for springtime to arrive.

> See how the white spirit presses us,
> Presses us, presses us, heavy and long,
> Presses us down to the frost-bitten earth.
> Alas, you are so heavy, your spirits so white.
> Alas, you are so cold, so cold, so cold.
> Cease, white spirits that fall from the skies.
> Cease so to crush us and keep us in dread.
> When will you vanish, and Seegwun [spring] return?

If you have long been attracted to the frog as your totem animal, you quite likely have always been intrigued by a study of the ancient wisdoms. You may also enjoy delving into the mysterious and the unknown. You are probably quite adaptable to sudden changes in your reality and in your environment, and while you pride yourself on your independence, you also have a great deal of empathy toward others.

If you have only recently received the frog as your totem animal and spirit helper, you may be about to undergo an unexpected change in your lifestyle or a transformation of a high spiritual nature. In either event, you may rely upon your frog to guide you safely through what might otherwise be a rather difficult transitional period. As a spirit helper, you may expect the frog to encourage you to spend a great deal more time in meditation and in a more active study of the ancient mysteries.

**Gazelle**—It has been said that to have a dream of a gazelle is to have had Cupid offer you a sign that you will soon fall in love.

If you have received the gazelle as your totem animal in a dream or a vision, you have received an ally that will keep you alert to any potential problems in your personal relationships and on the job. The grace that a gazelle represents in its physical environment will also become increasingly yours in social situations and in group activities. The gazelle functions best in partnerships or in communal activities and appreciates being able to rely on the herd for massed power and strength.

Your gazelle spirit helper will be of great assistance in enabling you to overcome any obstacles or hurdles in your lifepath. It will offer you a great sense of persistence and concentrated purpose. Your gazelle totem animal will be a reliable ally in helping you to achieve reasonable goals.

**Giraffe**—Among many African tribes, the giraffe is a symbol of friendship. Perhaps because the giraffe is essentially mute, it cannot "talk" too much and get into trouble.

If you have long been attracted to the giraffe as your totem animal, you are probably an easygoing, friendly person who enjoys relationships of long duration. You probably aren't much for formal occasions, preferring the casual company of a few good friends.

If you have just received the giraffe as your totem animal in a dream or a vision, you may have been given this energy to help you to relax and to become more sincere in your personal relationships. Perhaps you've been a bit too uptight both in your professional environment and in your family life. The giraffe will be a spirit helper that will greatly assist you in alleviating stress in your own life and helping you to eliminate the stressful situations that you may have been causing in the lives of others. As a traditional symbol of friendship, your spirit helper will never fail to be a good friend to you on your path toward ever-greater spiritual development.

**Goat**—As one of the earliest of all domesticated animals, perhaps second only to the dog, the goat has never been granted the status of friend and companion enjoyed by the canine species. Throughout the Hebrew and Mediterranean cultures, the goat was a favorite sacrificial animal, and in European lore, it stands as a symbol of unbridled lechery and even as Satan himself. Perhaps the unkindest cut came when Jesus related the parable of how one day God would separate the sheep from the goats.

The horned and hoofed woodland god Pan was among the very oldest of Greek deities. Today when we speak of "pantheism" we are referring to an identification of God with nature or with the universe. Our modern word "panic" hearkens back to the terrible cry of Pan that magically removed his enemies' strength and left them confused and helpless. Pan, with his goat's hindquarters and hoofs and his behorned skull, also became a model for the medieval European's Horned God of the Witches.

Among the Scandinavians, the goat was given special status not only because of the milk, cheese, and meat that it contributed to their survival during the harsh winters, but also because the giant, red-bearded god Thor rode with his mighty hammer in a cart pulled by goats.

The goat is the sign of Capricorn, December 22 to January 20, in the zodiac. Those born under this sign are thought to be industrious, economical individuals with great powers of endurance.

If you have long identified with the goat as your totem animal or if you have recently become drawn to it during a dream or a vision, you have chosen a spirit ally who will persist in assisting you to achieve whatever goals you wish to pursue. This spirit helper may have come to you to help you exercise more discernment in your relationships. Perhaps you need to know when to cease "butting" your head against brick walls.

**Goose**—Far more than a quaint symbol for children's nursery stories, Mother Goose was the great mother who laid the Golden Egg that hatched Ra, the sun god, into the world. In other even earlier versions of creation, Mother Goose laid the egg from which the entire planet emerged. For the Hindu, the goose represents Brahma and the principle of creation. In traditional depictions even today, Mother Goose always wears the pointed hat of the Egyptian ruler, the Witch, the wise woman, and she is never without her wand.

In the Middle Ages, the Jews believed anyone who killed a goose during Tevat and Shevat, the tenth and eleventh lunar months of the Hebrew calendar (mid-December through mid-February), placed himself at great risk unless he ate at least a part of the fowl he had slaughtered. Geese were associated with witchcraft, and it was said that at some specific time during those two months, demons would attack anyone who killed a goose. Since no one knew for certain the precise moment, geese were avoided for the entire period.

From the shamanistic perspective, the fairy tale that tells of Jack climbing the beanstalk to the giant's kingdom in the sky to steal the goose that laid the golden eggs is a symbolic representation of the Shaman who rises to the dimension of the Grandparents to earn the golden treasure of awareness.

For the Chinese, the goose symbolizes traditional values and fidelity, and a pair of geese is a welcome wedding present. In Christian tradition, the goose is the animal totem of three saints, Werburga, Brigid, and Martin.

If you've always been attracted to the goose as your totem animal, you are quite likely a person who cherishes the traditional values of your ancestral heritage. You are probably attracted to activities that center around your home, your community, and your school or church. A solid family life is especially important to you.

As a spirit helper, you may always rely on the goose for inspiration, guidance, and stability. You will gain strength from this ally as you spend time in the Silence.

**Grasshopper/Cricket**—These two leaping insects are presented here together because they are very often interchangeable in folk traditions around the world. Interestingly, although these tiny creatures can become king-sized pests and destroy entire crops and the livelihood of entire communities, from ancient Egypt to contemporary China, they represent happiness, good fortune, and a long life.

If the grasshopper/cricket appeals to you as a totem animal, you probably enjoy singing, dancing, and having a good time. You are open-minded and quite likely completely free of prejudice regarding gender, ethnic groups, or religions.

As a spirit helper, you can rely on your guide to help you lighten up when you grow overly concerned about matters that are not as serious as you believe them to be.

**Hawk**—In Egypt, hawks were kept in the temple of the sun god where the deity Horus was represented as a man with a hawk's head encircled by the disk of the sun. In Egyptian lore, the hawk came to symbolize the soul in its flight to the afterlife.

The Greeks considered the hawk sacred to the Great Light. The Romans associated the bird with Jupiter, father of the gods, and referred to the hawk as the Great Light of the Father.

The Ioway tribe so revered a particular species of hawk that they only killed it on rare occasions in order to obtain certain portions of its body to place with their most sacred medicines. The Shamans of the tribe believed that the hawk had a supernatural faculty that enabled it to remain indefinitely on the wing and to fly directly to the land of the Grandparents.

In the Medicine Wheel Zodiac, the red-tailed hawk is the totem animal for those born March 19 to April 19. Hawk people are thought to be adventurous and assertive, perhaps a bit headstrong, but always ones to cherish their freedom.

If the Hawk is your animal totem, you probably enjoy a very active dreamlife, perhaps returning almost nightly with messages from the Great Mystery. If you have only recently acquired the Hawk as your spirit helper, you may expect to begin receiving much more profound dream visions. You will also probably start to notice a somewhat dramatic increase in your psychic abilities.

As a spirit ally, you may rely on your hawk to be your trustworthy guide into the Silence. It will be of utmost importance to Hawk that you proceed on your earthwalk with spiritual balance.

**Horse**—In ancient Babylon, the horse was identified with the god Zu. The Greek word for horse is *ikkos,* the "great light," and they placed their god of wisdom in a chariot drawn by four fiery horses. The Hebrew word for horse means "to explain," thus equating the animal with the human intellect. The Latin *equus* resolves into the light of the great mind or soul.

To the ancient Vikings, the god Odin rode a swift horse across the sky and down into the realm of death. Many of the old Germanic tribes used horses for purposes of divination, believing the sacred beasts to be more in contact with the gods than were the priests.

Charlemagne presented his four sons with the magical talking horse Bayard, whose back could stretch from single saddle to accommodate all four of its masters.

Although the creature had been predicted by many Native American prophets, few tribespeople were prepared for their first encounter with the awesome animal that Coronado and the Spanish conquistadors brought to the plains in 1541. The eastern tribes and the Iroquois Confederacy did not have their visions of the strange beast realized until the early 1600s. Because the Blackfeet had no words to describe such animals and because they thought that the weird four-leggeds the armored and bearded strangers sat astride looked more like elk than anything else, they called them Medicine Elk.

The horse soon became a sacred and prized possession of the Native American people, just as it had been to the tribes of Europe and Asia.

For many Native American tribes, to see a vision of a great, white horse is to have seen the symbol of Death coming to take you to the land of the Grandparents. The association of a white horse with such an ethereal and holy task seems to have assumed the status of a universal image.

The Mohammedans have their *Al Borak,* a milk-white steed whose single stride can propel him as far as the farthest range of human vision. Slavic legends tell of Prince Slugobyl, who enlists the aid of the Invisible Knight and his horse Magu (magus, wizard), a magical, white horse with a golden mane.

Kwan-yin in China and Kuannan in Japan materialize as white horses. The Hindu god Vishnu's final manifestation will occur when he reappears on a white horse with a drawn sword to restore the order of righteousness. The Book of Revelation says that Christ shall return riding upon a white horse and leading armies of righteousness seated upon white horses.

In the Chinese zodiac, those born in the year of the horse are regarded as popular and attractive to the opposite sex, but inclined to be impatient.

If you have cherished the horse as your totem animal for many years, you have learned to appreciate your spirit helper's strength and intense desire to accomplish more things at a time than may seem possible. In addition to being able to infuse your physical body with energy and endurance, this animal guide also has the ability to transport you to ever-higher levels of awareness.

Don't be reluctant to ride your winged steed to explore worlds and dimensions beyond the ordinary. You need not fear becoming lost in other realities when you have such a trustworthy spiritual ally at your side.

**Leopard**—It was the Hebrew prophet Jeremiah who first warned us that a leopard cannot change his spots, and most of the world has been distrusting the big cat ever since. In Christian lore, the leopard symbolized lust and cruelty. When Medieval painters were creating those grim scenes of Judgment Day, the leopard came to symbolize Satan, hungrily devouring the souls of the damned.

It was in ancient Egypt that the big cat felt appreciated, for there the leopard was regarded as an aspect of divinity and associated with Osiris. The Chinese respect the leopard as a great warrior and use its image as a symbol of ferocity. For many African tribes, the leopard is a totem animal who is believed to guide the spirits of the dead to their rest.

If you only recently received the leopard in a dream or a vision as your totem animal, you may have been a somewhat shy person who has been reluctant to be an active participant in the competitive flow of life. Leopard may well have come to you to assist you in becoming more active and aggressive.

Don't be concerned, however, that this spirit helper will push you too quickly into the limelight. Leopard is reserved and dignified and not at all interested in the flashy or the superficial. This totem guide will help you to set obtainable goals—and then achieve them.

**Lion**—The "King of the Beasts," universally linked with royalty, strength, and courage, the lion is usually associated with masculine representations of the sun god in Greece and Rome. However, in the Middle East and Egypt the lion is more frequently represented as a woman. Sphinxlike, both nurturer and destroyer, the goddesses Sekhmet, Ishtar, Astarte, and Cybele rode lions, drove lions, or bore leonine features.

As might be supposed, the lion is a totem animal for many African tribes, and there are numerous well-established rituals for coexisting with the big cat. Its flesh is considered a potent food and medicinal cure. To eat its heart is to endow the feasting warrior with the strength and courage of the mighty beast itself.

The lion is the symbol of the tribe of Judah and of the Davidic line. It was a Hebrew belief that lions would not attack humans unless they were starving, thus providing further indication of their nobility and general goodwill. The milk of a lioness was thought to have potent healing properties. In earlier times, the angel Uriel would manifest as a lion and descend from heaven to eat the sacrificial offerings left in the Temple.

In alchemical traditions, white gold is called the "lion of metals." In Medieval esoteric literature, the lion, "king of beasts," symbolized the earthly opponent of the eagle, "lord of the skies." Both represented the masculine principle.

In the Christian tradition, both St. Mark and St. Jerome are symbolized by their animal totem the lion.

If you have had the lion as your totem animal for many years, you have quite likely been told since your childhood that you are a natural leader and organizer. If you have only recently accepted the lion as your spirit helper during a dream or a vision quest, you may expect that you are about to be promoted to a position requiring a bit more of an assertive personality than you have previously exhibited.

With Lion as your ally you will continually be placed in situations that will stretch your talents and broaden your horizon. You need never fear, however, that your spirit helper will put you in a problem area that will be over your head or beyond the grasp of your abilities. And you may always draw upon your totem animal's generous reserve of wisdom and enthusiasm.

**Lizard**—For many Native American tribes, the lizard is the gatekeeper to the dream world.

In the South Pacific, the little reptile is considered a messenger of the gods or even a minor deity. Numerous tales in folklore depict lizards as the ancestors of humans. The lizard's practice of shedding its skin makes it an almost universal symbol for regeneration.

If you have accepted the lizard as your totem animal, you have undoubtedly already discovered an enriched dreamlife. If you and Lizard have been connected for many years, you have learned the value of this spirit helper as a messenger from the Great Mystery and as a very reliable prophet of major events in your life. You should not become so dependent upon Lizard that you neglect your own time in the Silence. If you come to rely too strongly on your spirit helper for all your spiritual insights, it will withdraw from you until you have once again set your feet firmly on the path of regular meditation and spiritual exercises.

This totem guide has truly entered your life to help you to help yourself, and if you develop a balanced partnership, you may expect miracles and wonders to be yours.

**Lynx**—The ancient Greeks attributed such powerful eyesight to the lynx that they believed the cat was even able to see through mountains.

European folklore thought the lynx to be a strange combination of dog and panther. By Medieval times, claims of the creature's bizarre biological makeup, coupled with its purported remarkable eyesight, made it a perfect symbolic representation of the supernatural composition and all-seeing powers of Christ.

Native Americans took note of the lynx's hypnotic eyes, with their magnetic powers of seduction, and translated that attribute into numerous folktales in which the cat convinces one of its "relatives" to come closer. In each instance, the hungry lynx, no longer in need of flattery or a hypnotic gaze, immediately devours the rabbit, the squirrel, the prairie dog—his alleged "kinsmen."

If the lynx has been your totem animal for quite some time, you have no doubt already benefited from its patience and its willingness to wait long periods of time to achieve worthwhile goals. Your spirit helper's desire for independence must also appeal to you.

With the Lynx as your ally, you need seldom fear the invasion of low-level entities. Your totem animal is very protective of its spiritual territory, and it will fiercely defend your psyche from attack by negative beings. Lynx also has a keen nose for deception and will warn you against the deceitful and the two-faced in your work environment and in your personal relationships.

**Monkey**—In esoteric writings, the monkey frequently represents the baser, or darker, side of the human psyche. At the same time, while coming dangerously close to degrading an individual, these same ambivalent, dualistic forces may unexpectedly enrich and strengthen the initiate.

Certain African tribes cherish the monkey as a totem animal and grow so fond of the primates that the eating of their flesh is forbidden.

Those born during the Year of the Monkey on the Chinese zodiac are said to be intelligent, amiable, and overachieving. The traditional Chinese also believe that the monkey is able to communicate with nature sprites, fairies, and sorcerers.

In Hindu tradition, Hanuman, the benevolent simian-god, befriends and assists Prince Rama in his adventures to rescue the fair Sita in the *Ramayana,* a classic work of early Indian poetry. Hanuman is generally regarded as a model of pious devotion.

The Japanese maintain that three mystic monkeys hold the key to right living on the earthplane—see no evil; hear no evil; speak no evil.

If you have chosen the monkey as your totem animal, you have an ally that is both creative and imaginative. Although this totem guide may bring with it a slight tendency for overstatement or the expression of extremes in artistic endeavors, a bit more time spent in the Silence will more than balance the flamboyance.

Monkey will also be able to lead you into a deeper study of the origin of the human species and an examination of the ancient wisdoms. The agile mentality of this spirit helper will provide you with inspiration and insight when you most need it.

**Mouse**—Among the Rio Grande villages in the Southwest, the Pueblo fear that one of the meanest tricks of witches is to cause a mouse to grow inside someone's stomach. In old German folklore, it was believed that witches created mice out of scraps of cloth.

In the Christian tradition, St. Gertrude of Nivelles is represented by her animal emblem of the mouse. St. Gertrude must have exorcised her mouse, for an old Christian folktale claimed that Satan invented the tiny four-legged to torment the other animals aboard Noah's ark. Another legend went that story one better by claiming that Satan himself became a mouse and tried to gnaw through the ark and sink it.

Among the many things that a mouse totem animal can bring to you is an appreciation of the importance of the smallest details. This spirit helper will alert you to the need for introspection and a careful self-examination of your strongest and weakest attributes.

If you have chosen the mouse as your totem animal, you have probably already learned to conduct your life in an attitude of trust in the Great Mystery. Although you may at first have considered the doorway to other dimensions to be too formidable to allow your passage, Mouse no doubt taught you that persistence and devotion will permit you to squeeze through the smallest access to awareness.

**Owl**—The old Roman word for owl is *strix,* the same as their word for witch. Throughout northern Europe, the owl is also associated with witchcraft. Wicca means "wise ones," and the Witches of this tradition emphasize the owl as one of their principal animal totems.

Universally, the owl is a symbol for wisdom, and it is the totem animal for such ancient goddesses as Athene, Lilith, and Blodeuwedd, the Welsh Virgin Goddess of spring. Tlazolteotl, the Aztec goddess, shepherded the souls of women who died in childbirth and had the owl and the snake as her totem animals.

To the Winnebago, the owl ruled the north, the land of the unknown, of cold, dark forests; of death. Many Native American tribes believed that if they heard an owl calling their name, they were soon to join the Grandparents in the spirit world. In Celtic lore, the owl was also the "corpse bird" that carried the recently deceased to the underworld.

In the Rio Grande area of the Southwest, owls were considered the familiar that witches prefer over black cats. If one heard an owl hooting above one's rooftop at night, it was certain that evil was soon to visit the home.

The Zuni believed that if a family incurred the wrath of a witch, the evilworker would plant owl feathers in their cornfield, thus summoning a strong wind to destroy the crop.

The Apaches kept a wary eye out for Big Owl, a bloodthirsty, evil giant who took the form of a huge owl and carried humans off to eat them.

Although the Japanese generally regard the owl as a wise and benevolent night creature, most of the cultures of Asia fear the bird as a demon of darkness that delights in carrying off human souls. Conversely, in the Polynesian tradition, the owl is a special protector in battles or danger and brings back to life any souls that may be lost and wandering.

If you have long cherished the owl as a totem animal, you are quite likely a student of the mysterious and the unknown who loves to ferret out clues to the unexplained enigmas of existence on the Earth Mother. You probably enjoy watching magicians perform their craft, and you may even be an amateur magician. Even your closest friends may consider you something of a paradox—on the one hand, you seem to worship logic and reason; on the other, you appear to prefer fantasy and the illogical.

With the owl as your spirit helper, you will not cease to explore the most distant perimeters of the unknown. And you will not cease spending an equal amount of time in the Silence, receiving messages from the Great Mystery.

**Rabbit**—Many of the Native American tribes revered the spirit entity of the Great Rabbit as a sacred teacher of skills, arts, and crafts—and even as a participant with the Great Mystery in the creation of humankind.

The ancient Britons relied upon the rabbit as an instrument of divination, along with the cock and the goose. While many farmers raised the three animals, it was unlawful to eat them. Their actions, feeding patterns, and sometimes their entrails, could only be used for purposes of seership.

In both Native American and African tribal folklore, the rabbit (hare) is a quick-witted, smooth-talking individual, who may be small in size, but who triumphs over his adversaries and predators by his wits. Because it is obvious that some cross-cultural collaboration contributed to the popularity of the Brer Rabbit tales in the famous Uncle Remus stories, even their official recorder, Joel Chandler Harris, speculated that rabbit as trickster very likely originated in Africa and was later adopted by Native American tribes.

Quite apart from tales of quick-witted rabbits, the tribal Shamans perceived the animal's well-known attributes of fertility and reproduction to be related to action, life, and growth. The rabbit's large, red eyes were representative of the living fire of blood and the essence of the life force that courses through every living creature. Its ability to change its gray coat to white in its winter transfiguration was quite likely associated in the Shaman's mind with the change from rain to snow, and thus the rabbit was allied with the spirits of thunder and storm. Its nimble and quick actions, its flying leaps, connected the rabbit to the miracle of unfettered upward movement shared with the birds. Even the name of Manabozho, the Iroquois' legendary culture hero, is derived from the words for "great" and for "rabbit."

Those born in the Year of the Rabbit in the Chinese zodiac are said to have begun their earthwalk in the luckiest of all signs. Rabbit people are acclaimed as talented, articulate, affectionate, and peaceful.

If you have chosen the rabbit as your totem animal, you have an ally that will always be there to assist you in speeding up processes that appear to be merely limping along. This spirit helper may surprise you with the philosophical depth it will lend to your thought patterns. The rabbit has been a survivor for centuries, and your totem guide's skill in helping you through the rough spots in your earthwalk will be greatly appreciated by you.

If the rabbit has only recently come to you as a totem animal, you may have too often adopted the role of a victim in personal and business relationships. Rabbit will guide you into a new mindset that will enable you to regain status without resorting to low-level negativity. Rabbit is the eternal optimist, and this spirit helper will not tolerate depression and defeatism.

**Rat**—The rat has been living under a stigma since its connection with the bubonic plague was established. In the fourteenth century, nearly a quarter of Europe's population was taken by the Black Death, and the rat has been a symbol of Death for at least four centuries.

And then, of course, there's the old sailor's adage about rats leaving a sinking ship before disaster strikes, which has made the rat synonymous with a traitor or a deserter. While the rat's cousin, the mouse, has conquered the world as a symbol of fun, fantasy, and frivolity, there is no Ricky Rat to compete with Mickey Mouse.

Those individuals born in the Year of the Rat in the Chinese zodiac are counted as people who are ambitious, yet honest, who are prone to spend their money too freely.

If you can move beyond the stigma associated with this large rodent, you will gain a totem animal that will aid you in establishing a comfortable and efficient home and help you courageously defend it against all external negativity. There is also a great deal of magical energy vibrating around this spirit helper, and you may be led into a more serious study of the ancient mysteries through its encouragement. Rat will also lend you the necessary energy to become a respected worker in the business environment. You will never be tempted to gamble or fritter away your salary, however. Rat will see to it that you make only wise investments that will benefit your home and family.

**Sheep**—Those who arrived on the Earth Mother in the Chinese zodiac's Year of the Sheep are classified as elegant, creative, and timid to the point of preferring anonymity.

The lamb became the totemic symbol of Christ, based on the Jewish tradition of sacrificing a first-born lamb at Passover. Since much earlier times, however, the lamb was a symbol of purity, innocence, and meekness, and it became a sacrificial surrogate for the sins of the shepherd and his people. The symbolic dualism of the lion and the lamb as extremes to be found on the human earthwalk has remained popular as an artistic theme. St. Agnes and St. John the Baptist have the lamb as their animal emblem.

If the sheep appeals to you as a totem animal, it may be because you find a certain strength in conformity or in working in groups. You may prefer a life as free of conflict, stress, and competition as possible. There is no question that this spirit helper will bring with it an aura of peace, but it will also encourage you to begin to become less vulnerable to the various slings and arrows of life on the earthplane and to become a bit more assertive both in the workplace and at home.

If you are in one of the service professions, you are bound to find the sheep a valuable totem guide, for it will give you the strength to continue to provide the care that you wish to lend to others. In a real sense, this spirit helper will forge a link with you that will transmit loving energy directly from the Great Mystery to your body, mind, and spirit, so that you may energize others.

**Snake**—Although the snake is feared and loathed throughout every culture around the planet where reptiles appear, it is among the most universally respected and sought-after of all animal totems. In ancient Egypt, the snake was regarded as a symbol of both immortality and death, and the pharaoh wore a snake emblem on his headdress as a mark of royalty and divinity. Apep was the Egyptian and Greek name for the Great Serpent of the Underworld. Ouroboros was the Greek name for the gigantic serpent coiled in the earth's womb.

Apollo, the Greek god of healing and medicine, was originally invoked and worshipped as a snake. In later times, Aesculapius, another deity associated with medicine, is said to have assumed serpentine form. His crest remains today as a symbol of the medical profession.

In Hindu mythology, Vishnu sleeps cradled in the folds of the great serpent Sesha. In the Hindu tradition, evil spirits are directed in their misdeeds by their leader, a great serpent.

In the Hebrew account of the fall from Paradise, the serpent was the king of beasts, walking on two legs, eating of the same food as Adam and Eve. However, when the serpent saw how the angels honored Adam, it became jealous of the human. For his part in the seduction and defilement of Eve, he is punished by having his arms and legs cut off and by being reduced to crawling on his belly throughout all time. In the Moslem tradition, Archangel Michael chops off the satanic serpent's legs with the sword of God. In Native American legends, such cultural heroes as Manabozho battle not one, but many serpent people, who seek to hold humans in bondage.

To the ancient people of Asia Minor, Ophion was the father of all humankind, the divine serpent who lived in the Tree of Life in the primal garden.

The brazen serpent that Moses raised in the wilderness was named Nehustan. The statue was destroyed by David's son Hezekiah when he ascended to the throne of Judah. Nehustan was quite likely descended from the Vedic serpent king Nahusha, ruler of all gods until Indra cast him down to the underworld.

Until the eighteenth century, Basilisk, a mythical snake so poisonous that it could kill its victims with a glance, was thought by Europeans to be a real serpent. The idea of Basilisk was probably inspired by the old Greek legend of the Gorgon, a female monster whose hair composed of writhing serpents was so frightening that to gaze upon her was to risk being turned into stone. The Japanese have their version of the Gorgon in Yama-uba, a terrifying demon who appears as a long-haired woman. Once Yama-uba sights her prey, her long tresses transform themselves into ravenous snakes which draw the victim into a mouth on the top of her head.

In ancient Mexico, Ciuacoatl, the Great Mother of men and gods, is represented as a serpent woman. Quetza-coatl, the great culture bearer, is depicted as a winged serpent. Among many African tribes, it is Aido Hwendo, the Rainbow Serpent, that supports the earth.

Father Charlevoix, an early French missionary to the eastern tribes of North America, remarked in his journals that there was no image that the Native American tribes marked upon their faces and other parts of their bodies more than that of the snake. Furthermore, according to the priest's observations, the Shamans had the secret of charming snakes, of benumbing them, "so that they take them alive, handle them, and put them in their bosom without receiving any hurt."

The rattlesnake was considered the chief of all serpents; and some tribes believed that in addition to delivering death via the strike of its deadly fangs, the "chief" could transmit diseases with but a glance of its beady eyes.

If a coiled rattlesnake should appear in the path of a warrior, he would freeze in his tracks, speak beseechingly to it, and offer it whatever gifts he had on his person that he hoped might propitiate the angry chief of snakes.

The Medicine Priests who walked unharmed among the rattlesnakes knew that the powerful essence of the Great Mystery moved through them. Those who had received the snake as a totem animal during the vision quest felt especially blessed. The Pueblo, Hopi, and Zuni tribes revered Horned Serpent and Horned Water Serpent as largely benevolent guardian spirits and prized snakes as totem animals and spirit helpers.

Shamans revered the snake for its great wisdom, and many believed that the serpent spoke a secret language of its own that no other animal was permitted to comprehend. According to many tribal legends, in the beginning time, humans and snakes could converse freely. Therefore, if one were powerfully attuned on the spirit level, he or she could still communicate with a snake on the telepathic level. If one could achieve this mind linkup, the serpent would reveal secrets of the future and other aspects of arcane knowledge.

The skin of the rattlesnake was used by nearly all Medicine Priests in some aspect of their rituals, and their rattles were often carried in the priests' sacred pouches.

Those born in the Year of the Snake in the Chinese zodiac are characterized as wise and intense, with a tendency to be vain about their physical beauty. The sign of the Snake in the Native American zodiac (October 23 to November 21) identifies a person who is charismatic, but difficult to comprehend.

The snake is the animal emblem for St. Patrick, whose victory over the serpents of Ireland is celebrated every March seventeenth.

If you accepted the snake as your totem animal some time ago, you have probably always been drawn to the strange, the mysterious, the unexplained. You have quite likely amassed a rather large library of esoteric and metaphysical works, and you are no doubt attracted to a study of ancient cultures and religions. Discoveries of unknown ruins of alleged prehistoric origins are certain to excite you.

If you have only recently received the snake as your spirit helper in a dream or a vision quest, your totem guide may have arrived to assist you in aspects of your personal transformation. Perhaps friends and family members have thought you a bit too impersonal, too indifferent, too "cold-blooded." Snake may have come into your life to help you to develop more sensitivity to others around you in your immediate environment.

When you enter the Silence with Snake as your ally, you are certain to go deep within and draw forth ancient wisdom teachings that will immediately be able to change your life for the better.

**Spider**—As a powerful totem animal in many cultures, the spider's act of weaving its web may serve as a symbol of the creative process, a warning of entanglement and deception, or a representation of the illusory spiral of reality.

In India, the spider is the emblem of Maya, the eternal weaver of illusion. In ancient Greece, the creature and its web was the totemic symbol of Athene, goddess of wisdom, and the Fates. In Egypt, the spider represented Neith, the Divine Mother.

The Cherokee have a folktale in which it was the spider that answered humankind's prayer for fire and brought the mystic energy on its gossamer web from the Spirit of Flame to the tribes of North America. Other Native American tribes depict the spider as the sacred weaver that spun the world into existence, and the industrious insect remains emblematic of the creative female force.

If you have recently received the spider as your totem animal, you have joined energies with an ally that will assist you in grasping the interworkings of personal dynamics more than ever before in your life. You will begin to have a completely new perspective on how seemingly disparate facets of your life are all woven together in intricate patterns with infinite possibilities. If you have been feeling somewhat dissociated from others and confused about what specific earthpath you should be following, your spirit helper will guide you to a much clearer understanding of your niche in life.

Spider will also assist you in perceiving the application of ancient wisdoms to your life today and help you to separate the webs of illusion and confusion from your worldview.

**Swan**—Since the days of the ancient Greeks, the swan has been a symbol of grace, beauty, chastity, and innocence—and at the same time, the fulfillment of desire. While the whiteness of the large bird bespeaks purity, in the Western world, the swan has remained an erotic symbol, with an extensive folklore of graceful swans that shape-shift into lovely maidens to marry and mate with human husbands.

In one of the most familiar of all Greek myths, the mighty Zeus disguises himself as a swan in order to seduce the goddess Leda. The result of their passion is the World Egg.

The heavenly Apsaras of Hindu mythology were lovely swan nymphs, and Krishna, a swan knight.

While the great majority of the Vikings' Valkyries flew above the battlefields in the black feathers of crows, certain of them chose cloaks of swan feathers in which to sing melodies that would cause confusion in enemy ranks. Other swan-cloaked Valkyries sang welcome hymns to those fallen warriors who must travel to the spirit world. In Christian tradition, the swan is the animal emblem for St. Hugh of Lincoln.

If you have discovered through dreams or a vision quest that the swan is your totem animal, you may have required a lively injection of confidence into your love life. Swan will definitely aid you in acquiring social skills and a distinctive style and poise that will have all of your old friends puzzled—and your new acquaintances impressed.

This spirit helper's specialty lies in the field of transformation, but that applies to the spirit as well as the body. Swan also has the ability to serve as a messenger to the mystical realms of the Great Mystery, so be certain to call upon your totem guide's energy before you enter the Silence.

**Tiger**—In those regions where the tiger is king of the beasts, he is spoken of with the same reverence and respect accorded the lion in his domain, and he is regarded as a similar symbol of nobility and strength. It does seem, though, that the tiger is considered a bit testier and harder for his human neighbors to please. There are innumerable rules with which one must comply to avoid incurring the big cat's displeasure.

In Malaysia, it is considered bad manners ever to mention the tiger by name. Euphemisms such as "behold the striped one," or "beware of old hair face," or "do not offend the one who roars" are carefully employed by those who share the jungle with the tiger. Those who really wish to play it safe simply address him as "Lord."

Europe must deal with its werewolves, but all of Asia has to face the grim nocturnal visitation of weretigers. And just as Native American Shamans or witches may favor the bodies of coyotes for shape-shifting excursions, the magicians of Asia prefer the swift-moving bulk of the tiger.

Those born in the Chinese zodiac's Year of the Tiger are said to be aggressive, courageous, candid, and sensitive.

In the traditions of China, the tiger, like the dragon, has both a dark and destructive side and a righteous and constructive side. By using the five tigers, mythic defenders against chaos, as designators of seasons, one could build a small Chinese Medicine Wheel: The center stone is the Yellow Tiger, Emperor of all other tigers and the element of earth; south is the Red Tiger, representing summer and the element of fire; north is the Black Tiger, symbolizing winter and the element of water; east finds the Blue Tiger ruling over spring, with its vegetation; and west is the White Tiger, reigning over autumn and the metals.

If you have long been attracted to the tiger as an animal totem, you are probably a firm believer in the old adage of a sound mind in a sound body. You may enjoy various sports activities, but you would rather play a hard and tough game than watch it on television or from the stands.

If this spirit helper has only recently come to you in a dream or a vision, you will notice an increase in your strength and endurance. At the same time, you will have a desire to pursue certain intellectual pursuits that have not previously appealed to you, and you may find yourself becoming much more politically active. With Tiger as your totem guide, you may feel encouraged to develop your abilities as a healer.

**Turtle**—The world that the Native American tribes knew existed on the back of a great turtle. All of North America, including Canada and Mexico, constitute that landmass that traditional Native Americans still refer to as Turtle Island. The Native Americans were not alone in awarding the honor of bearing the weight of the Earth Mother to the turtle, for both the Chinese and the Hindu cultures also award Brother Tortoise the task of balancing the globe on his back.

The turtle is the animal totem that represents peace on the earth-walk. As Grandmother Twylah explained it, "The turtle rattle is emblematic of peace of mind, and it is used in the dances to help portray happiness. Peace is a state of mind. It can be attained through daily learning experiences. We must learn and understand how to walk in balance on the Pathway of Peace."

In China, and among a number of African tribes, the turtle is emblematic of the female principle. At the same time, the Chinese saw the turtle, with its hard shell, as the perfect totem animal of the invincible warrior. Conversely, among the Aztecs, the turtle was symbolic of the braggart and coward, who talks tough, but has a soft underbelly. In numerous cultures the turtle is a symbol of longevity.

In certain metaphysical thought systems, the turtle represents the slowly developing aspects of physical evolution in contrast to a rapid burst of spiritual evolution, as might be symbolized by an eagle or a hawk.

If the turtle is the animal totem of your choice, you have selected a spirit helper that will greatly assist you in a profound study of the ancient wisdoms. It may well be that you have needed your totem guide's steady persistence to guide you in your spiritual search and to temper your impatience and your tendency to require instant reinforcement. It may be Turtle's job to help you become more grounded.

This spirit helper can also bring stability to weakened relationships and help you to bolster a family life that may have begun to deteriorate. Ask Turtle to help you form a true respect for the Earth Mother and a renewed appreciation of the feminine principle.

**Whale**—In the language of symbolism, this large aquatic mammal has variously represented the earth, the physical body of a man, and the final resting place of all humans, the grave. In the mythology of some cultures, the whale replaces the more common image of the turtle as the creature that supports the Earth Mother in space.

Queen Semiramis, legendary founder of the city of Babylon, was the daughter of the fish goddess, Derceto, who appeared as a whale, the Great Fish.

There is no St. Jonah, but the whale is the animal emblem for St. Malo and St. Brendan. In later Christian literature, authors adapted Matthew's use of Jonah's sojourn in the whale's belly as symbolic of Christ's three days in the tomb and imaginatively transfigured the whale's mighty jaws to represent the gates of Hell.

If you have only recently received the whale as your totem animal through a dream or a vision, you perhaps noticed that certain of your ESP abilities, especially that of telepathy, began to increase dramatically. If the whale has been your spirit helper for quite some time, you are very likely a generous person with keen humanitarian interests and a strong belief in the basic moral teachings expressed in most of the world's religions.

This totem guide will encourage you to pursue your spiritual development and, at the same time, to maintain a good balance between your family life and your responsibilities in the workplace.

**Wolf**—For many traditional people, Wolf is the sage, the Grand Teacher. In the *Wolf Lodge Journal*, Ghost Wolf reminds us that the Old Ones have told stories about the beginning time when it was Wolf who taught humans the ways of living in harmony:

"It was Wolf who taught us how to form community upon this Earth, for Wolves have an intuitive knowledge of order . . . and they possess the ability to survive change intact. Wolf medicine is very ancient and born of living experience. Wolf will look deep into your heart and share the greatest of knowledge, but will demand full participation and absolute sincerity. Wolf . . . will rekindle old memories within your soul . . . Wolf medicine can make you whole."

One of the most popular of all clan and totem animals among Native Americans, the wolf was also the sacred totem of many European clans during the Middle Ages. Pick up the telephone book from any major city in North America or Europe and count the number of names under Wolf, Wolfberg, Wolfe, Wolfenbarger, Wolfgang, Wolfman, Wolfsen, Wolfstein, and so on.

According to Norse mythology, Fenrir, the great wolf of the North, will be set free on doomsday to swallow the sun. Just as many Viking warriors, *berserkrs,* wore a bear-shirt into battle to demonstrate their ferocity, so did many don the wolf-coat to warn the enemy that they might change into wolves before their eyes and become even more vicious in their attack.

A quick reading of history would indicate that in order to found a city, an empire, or a country, it is a prerequisite to have a wolf somewhere in the family tree. Romulus and Remus, the legendary twin founders of Rome, were suckled by a she-wolf. Tu Kueh, fabled founder of the Turkish nation, later married the divine she-wolf who suckled and reared him.

Siegfried, one of the mightiest of the Teutonic heroes, who conquered dragons, the heart of the Queen of the Valkyries, and a number of warrior opponents, had been nursed by a she-wolf after his mother died in childbirth.

Wolf Moondance, a Shaman of the Osage people, says that the parenting instinct is very strong in wolves. They are natural mothers and fathers. "When you are in need, when you are in danger or feeling separated and abandoned, you can transmit psychic energy and pull to you to the energy of the She-Wolf. You can allow the feeling of that desire to draw you to the principle of the mother embracing the child."

In the Christian tradition, the wolf is the emblem for St. Francis of Assisi, St. Edmund of East Anglia, and St. Wolfgang.

If the wolf has been designated as your totem animal through dreams or vision quest, be assured that you have a spirit helper that will always back you up, regardless of the consequences. This totem guide is known for its extraordinary powers of endurance, and it will willingly grant those strengths to you. Wolf is the Great Parent, the Great Teacher, the Great Friend, and your spirit helper will expect you to carry on its traditions and to fulfill your own responsibilities to your family, your community, your friends, and those less fortunate than you who need your help. Wolf will tolerate no shirking of duty, so while you have a fierce guardian on twenty-four hour notice, you also have an example of trust and nobility to respect and emulate.

# Bibliography

Alexander, Hartley Burr. *The World's Rim*. Lincoln: University of Nebraska Press, 1953.

———. *Manito Masks*. New York: E. P. Dutton, 1925.

Beckwith, Martha. *Hawaiian Mythology*. Honolulu: University of Hawaii Press, 1970.

Bierhorst, John. *The Mythology of Mexico and Central America*. New York: William Morrow and Company, 1990.

———. *The Mythology of South America*. New York: William Morrow and Company, 1988.

Brinton, Daniel G. *The Lenape and Their Legends*. St. Clair Shores, MI: Scholarly Press, 1972.

Brown, Joseph Epes. *The Sacred Pipe*. Baltimore: Penguin Books, 1972.

Campbell, Joseph. *The Hero with a Thousand Faces*. Princeton: Princeton University Press, 1968.

Carver, Jonathan. *Three Years Travels Through the Interior Parts of North America for More Than Five Thousand Miles*. Philadelphia: Key & Simon, 1796.

Cirlot, J. E. *A Dictionary of Symbols*. New York: Barnes & Noble, 1971.

Courlander, Harold. *Tales of Yoruba Gods and Heroes*. Greenwich: Fawcett Publications, 1974.

———. *The Fourth World of the Hopis*. Greenwich: Fawcett Publications, 1972.

Crim, Keith, general editor. *The Perennial Dictionary of World Religions*. San Francisco: HarperCollins, 1989.

Davidson, H. R. Ellis. *Myths and Symbols in Pagan Europe*. Syracuse: Syracuse University Press, 1988.

Dossey, Larry, M.D. *Recovering the Soul*. New York: Bantam Books, 1989.

Douglas, Mary. *Natural Symbols*. New York: Pantheon, 1970.

Eliade, Mircea. *The Quest*. Chicago: University of Chicago Press, 1969.

Eliot, Alexander. *The Universal Myths*. New York: Meridian, 1990.

Emerson, Ellen Russell. *Indian Myths*. Minneapolis: Ross & Haines, 1965.

Fergusson, Erna. *Dancing Gods*. Albuquerque: University of New Mexico Press, 1966.

Fletcher, Alice C., and La Flesche, Francis. *The Omaha Tribe*. Lincoln: University of Nebraska Press, 1972.

Gaster, Theodor H. *The New Golden Bough*. New York: Criterion Books, 1959.

Gonzalez, Magda, and Gonzalez, J. A. *Star-Spider Speaks: The Teachings of the Native American Tarot*. Stamford, CT: U.S. Games Systems, 1990.

Gordon, Stuart. *The Encyclopedia of Myths and Legends*. London: Headline, 1993.

Hamilton, Charles, editor. *Cry of the Thunderbird*. Norman: University of Oklahoma Press, 1972.

Hays, H. R. *From Ape to Angel*. New York: Alfred A. Knopf, 1958.

Hoebel, E. Adamson. *The Cheyennes*. New York: Holt, Rinehart and Winston, 1960.

Jones, Alison. *Dictionary of World Folklore*. New York: Larousse, 1995.

Kluckhohn, Clyde, and Leighton, Dorothea. *The Navaho*. Garden City: Anchor Books, 1962.

Kluckhohn, Clyde. *Navaho Witchcraft*. Boston: Beacon Press, 1967.

Lissner, Ivar. *Man, God and Magic*. New York: G. P. Putnam's Sons, 1961.

Medicine Hawk & Grey Cat. *American Indian Ceremonies*. New Brunswick, NJ: Inner Light Publications, 1990.

Middleton, John, editor. *Magic, Witchcraft, and Curing*. Garden City: The Natural History Press, 1967.

Nequatewa, Edmund. *Truth of a Hopi*. Flagstaff, AZ: Northland Press, 1967.

Newcomb, Franc Johnson. *Hosteen Klah*. Norman: University of Oklahoma Press, 1964.

Parrot, Fred J. *Introduction to African Arts*. New York: Arco, 1972.

Parsons, Elsie Clews, editor. *American Indian Life*. Lincoln: University of Nebraska Press, 1973.

Pukui, Mary Kawena; Haertig, E. W., M.D.; and Lee, Catherine A. *Nana I Ke Kumu (Look to the Source)*. Honolulu: Hui Hanai, 1972.

Red Fox, William. *The Memoirs of Chief Red Fox*. Greenwich: Fawcett Publications, 1972.

Roderick, Timothy. *The Once Unknown Familiar*. St. Paul: Llewellyn, 1994.

Rose, Ronald. *Living Magic*. New York: Rand-McNally, 1956.

Schoolcraft, Henry R. *The Hiawatha Legends*. Marquette, MI: Avery Color Studios, 1994.

Sejourne, Laurette. *Burning Water*. Berkeley: Shambhala, 1976.

Simek, Rudolf. *Dictionary of Northern Mythology*. Rochester, NY: Boydell & Brewer, 1993.

Simmons, Marc. *Witchcraft in the Southwest*. Flagstaff, AZ: Northland Press, 1974.

Stands in Timber, John and Liberty, Margaret. *Cheyenne Memories*. Lincoln: University of Nebraska Press, 1972.

Steiger, Brad. *Kahuna Magic*. West Chester, PA: Whitford Press, 1981.

———. *The Gods of Aquarius*. New York: Harcourt Brace Jovanovich, 1976.

———. *Medicine Talk*. Garden City: Doubleday & Company, 1975.

———. *Medicine Power*. Garden City: Doubleday & Company, 1974.

Stevens, Dr. Anthony. *Archetypes*. New York: Quill, 1983.

Stoutenburgh, John, Jr., *Dictionary of the American Indian*. New York: Philosophical Library, 1970.

Sun Bear, Wind, Wabun & Shawnodese. *Dreaming with the Wheel*. New York: Fireside, 1994.

Sun Bear, Wabun, Nimimosha. *The Bear Tribe's Self Reliance Book*. Spokane: Bear Tribe Publishing, 1977.

Sun Bear (as told to) Wabun & Weinstock, Barry. *The Path of Power*. Spokane: Bear Tribe Publishing, 1983.

Thompson, Stith (selected and annotated by) *Tales of the North American Indian*. Bloomington and London: Indiana University Press, 1966.

Tyler, Hamilton A. *Pueblo Gods and Myths*. Norman: University of Oklahoma Press, 1964.

Unterman, Alan. *Dictionary of Jewish Lore & Legend*. London: Thames and Hudson, 1991.

Walker, Barbara G. *The Woman's Encyclopedia of Myths and Secrets*. San Francisco: Harper & Row, 1983.

Weltfish, Gene. *The Lost Universe*. New York: Ballantine, 1971.

Willmington, H. L. *Willmington's Book of Bible Lists*. Wheaton: Tyndale, 1987.

# For Additional Information on Totem Readers or Leaders of Native American Workshops

Grandmother Twylah
Seneca Historical Society
Cattaraugus Reservation
12199 Brant Reservation Road
Irving, New York 14081

Numerous kinds of activities and services are available to the serious student of
Native American religious and philosophical concepts through the Seneca
Historical Society. Interested individuals should always write in advance of their
visit.

The Bear Tribe
P.O. Box 959
Canandaigua, NY 14424

The vision of Sun Bear lives on in the work of the Bear Tribe. Medicine Wheel
gatherings are conducted throughout the United States and in Europe. Newsletters
and other publications are available.

L. Dean Woodruff
5785 Tee Pee Lane
Las Vegas, Nevada 89199

Woodruff is a reader of totemic symbols, who sees clients by appointment.

Julia C. White
3285 Park Lane
Long Beach, California 90807

Julia White conducts seminars and workshops on a wide range of Native American
concepts, including the acquisition of totemic symbols and spirit helpers.

Lawrence Kennedy & Sandra Sitzmann
Starline Unlimited
1–2nd Avenue East, Suite C–234
Polson, Montana 59860

The Starline Center assists individuals with the seeking and interpretation of their
totemic symbols and their ecological balance.

Mary Elizabeth Thunder
Rt. 1, Box 87C
West Point, Texas 78963

Mary Elizabeth Thunder conducts a wide range of Native American seminars, workshops, and visionary activities. It is necessary to write before your visit to the ranch.

Tara Sutphen
Valley of the Sun
Box 38
Malibu, California 90265

Tara Sutphen conducts seminars with her husband, Dick, throughout the United States. Her shamanic tapes are available with the accompaniment of beautiful, clay-flute music and effects created especially for her guided meditations.

Brad and Sherry Steiger
Timewalker
Box 434
Forest City, Iowa 50436

Interested parties may send a stamped, self-addressed business envelope to receive a list of books, tapes, and other items of eclectic shamanism.

Tara C. Buckland
P.O. Box 982
Wooster, OH 44691

Beverly Hale Watson
2120 Pine Thicket
Bedford, TX 76021

Laura Day
P.O. Box 1682
La Salle, IL 61301

Esther Hamel
c/o Ponderosa Publishers
2037 Airport Road
St. Ignatius, MT 59865

Sharon Rammon
E9128 South Avenue
Reedsburg, WI 53959